Table of Contents

Seafood

Beef and Pork

Sandwiches

Pasta and Meatless Entrees

Soups and Salads

Snacks

Introduction

Welcome to *The College Cookbook*. My name is James Warren, and I am an actual college student at Texas Tech. Most people think college cooking is throwing some ramen in the microwave and calling it a day. The average student's diet is pathetic and filled with processed foods that provide little to no nutritional value. While students might be able to get away with it now, there will be a day when that lifestyle catches up with them.

This book focuses on 3 key features.

Simplicity

While I was writing recipes, I realized that some are actually really difficult to follow. So I decided to make videos that show all of the challenging steps in the cookbook. This will save you much headache and confusion when trying to decipher what you are supposed to do.

Health

Being the health nut I am, each recipe has the exact nutrition facts. I went a step above and added the exact nutrition fact from each ingredient, so you know exactly where all of the calories are coming from.

Quality

I have made sure that every recipe in this book has been tested and tried by someone other than myself. This recipe book has 101 recipes, but I probably weeded through over 200 to get here.

Nutrition

In a world of processed and packaged foods, most college students don't know how to eat right. Their diets consist of eating ramen, cheese quesadillas, and cereal. Few eat healthy due to a lack of money, knowledge, and a desire to eat right.

While you might be able to get away with eating terribly now, one day it will catch up to you; just ask your parents. Below, I have simplified the basics to help you understand how certain foods impact your health. The first step is understanding calories.

Calories

A calorie is a unit for measuring energy. We use calories to determine the amount of energy in food. When you hear something has 100 calories, it describes how much energy your body gets from that food.

Calories are very important because it is the secret to weight. No matter how much you think it is impossible to lose weight, it's not. Gaining and losing weight is literally a science. The most important part of calories is understanding your maintenance calories. Your maintenance calories are the number of calories you need to eat to maintain your weight. The average person's maintenance calories are between 1500-2500 calories.

To lose weight, you need to eat under your maintenance calories.

To maintain weight, you need to eat your maintenance calories.

To gain weight, you need to eat more than your maintenance calories.

So if your maintenance calories = 2,000

Eat < 2,000 calories to lose weight.

Eat 2,000 calories to maintain weight.

Eat > 2,000 calories to gain weight.

Scan the QR code below to find your maintenance calories.

There are many different types of calories, and not all are created equal. There are 3 main types of calories.

- Carbohydrates
- Fats
- Protein

Carbohydrates

Carbohydrates are molecules that have carbon, hydrogen, and oxygen atoms. They consist of sugar, starches, and fiber. The main purpose of carbohydrates is to provide energy for our body. Carbs come in a wide array of foods like bread, pasta, potatoes, chips, soda, oats, fruits, vegetables, and much more. Each gram of carbohydrates contains 4 calories.

Simple carbs

Simple Carbs (also known as refined carbs) mainly includes processed sugar and refined grains. They have been stripped of their nutrients, which is why they are considered empty calories. Simple carbs lead to spikes in blood sugar and insulin levels.

Simple carbs include:

- White bread
- White rice
- Sugar
- Candy
- Cookies
- Chips
- Soda

Complex Carbs

Complex Carbs are packed with nutrients and digest much slower than simple carbs. Unlike simple carbs, complex carbs are only made of starches and fiber.

Complex carbs include:

- Fruits
- Vegetables
- Whole grains
- Oats
- Rice

Fats

Fats give you energy while helping your body absorb vitamins and minerals. Every gram of fat contains 9 calories. Many people believe diets with little to no fat are good; however, this could not be further from the truth. While some types of fat are bad for you, 20-40% of your daily calorie intake should consist of healthy fats (unless you're on the keto diet or something like that).

There are 3 types of fats:

Unsaturated Fat

This type of fat is liquid at room temperature. Unsaturated fat can improve blood cholesterol levels, ease inflammation, stabilize heart rhythms, and much more.

Unsaturated fat is primarily found in vegetable oil, nuts, and seeds. There are two types of unsaturated fat, and they are both healthy.

Monounsaturated fat

This fat has one double bond.
Examples:

- Avocado
- Olive and peanut oil
- Almonds
- Hazelnuts
- Pecans
- Pumpkin and sesame seeds

Polyunsaturated fat

This fat has 2-6 double bonds.
Examples:

- Sunflower and flaxseed oils
- Walnuts
- Flax and Chia seeds
- Fish

You can't really go wrong with unsaturated fats. I recommend that 20-30% of your calories come from unsaturated fats (for most diets).

Saturated Fats

This fat is solid at room temperature. Saturated fats are in  between the great unsaturated fats and the evil trans fats. There are many debates on whether saturated fats cause heart disease and high cholesterol.

As long as you do not consume too much of them, you will be fine. Saturated fats are found in animal products like milk, cheese, meat, and tropical oils, including coconut and palm oil.
Examples:

- Bacon
- Red meat
- Cheese
- Butter
- Regular milk
- Coconut oil

Your saturated fat intake should stay under 10% of your daily calories.

.

Trans Fats

Trans fat is made by heating liquid vegetable oils in the presence of hydrogen gas and a catalyst. This process is called hydrogenation which increases the fat's shelf life. Trans fat is really bad for you, and you want to consume as little as possible.
Examples:

- French fries
- Donuts
- Cookies
- Coffee creamer
- Pizza
- Microwave popcorn

Protein

Protein is a macronutrient made up of chemical building blocks called amino acids. Amino acids build up your bones, repair your muscles, and help create your enzymes and hormones. Your body needs protein to grow and repair cells. Each gram of protein contains 4 calories.

It is important that your body gets enough protein every day. The recommended daily average protein intake is:

.6-.8 grams per pound for women

.8-1.2 grams per pound for men

So a 100-pound woman should eat 60-80 grams of protein per day.

And a 200-pound man should eat 160-240 grams of protein per day.

Examples of protein include:

- Chicken
- Steak
- Fish
- Greek yogurt
- Eggs

Cutting Methods

Below are some basic cutting techniques that every chef should know how to do.

Garlic

Scan the QR code below to see how to mince garlic.

Scan Me

Onion

Scan the QR code below to see how to dice an onion.

Scan Me

Onion

Scan the QR code below to see how slice an onion.

Scan Me

Onion

Scan the QR code below to see how to roughly chop an onion.

Scan Me

Roma Tomato

Scan the QR code below to see how dice to a Roma tomato.

Scan Me

Roma Tomato

Scan the QR code below to see how to slice a Roma tomato.

Scan Me

Bell Pepper

Scan the QR code below to see how to dice a Bell pepper.

Scan Me

Bell Pepper

Scan the QR code below to see how to chop and slice a Bell pepper.

Scan Me

Green Onions

Scan the QR code below to see how to cut a green onion.

Scan Me

Avocado

Scan the QR code below to see how to cut an avocado.

Scan Me

Breakfast

Ginger Apple Smoothie

 SERVES 1

🕐 TOTAL TIME: 5 min

- Water- 1/3 cup or 75 ml
- Spinach- 2 cups or 56g
- Cucumber- 1 cup or 120g
- Mint leaves- 1 teaspoon or .66g
- Ginger- ¼ teaspoon or .5g
- ½ of an apple
- 4-5 ice cubes

1. Add everything into a blender and blend.

Blend everything together for about 30 seconds and enjoy!

Breakfast		79
Spinach 2 cup		14
Chopped Cucumber (Peeled). Chopped Cucumber (Peeled)., 1 cup		16
Apple 0.5 medium		47
Ginger Simply Organic, 0.5 gram(s)		1

	Total
Carbohydrates (17g)	82%
Fat (0g)	6%
Protein (2g)	12%

Nutrition Facts

Calories 79

Fat 0g

Saturated fat 0g

Carbohydrates 17g

Fiber 5g

Sugar 12g

Protein 2g

Sodium 51mg

Pineapple Kale Smoothie

 SERVES 1

🕐 TOTAL TIME: 5 min

- Unsweetened Almond milk- 1 cup or 240 ml
- Pineapple juice- ½ cup or 120 ml
- Kale- 1 cup or 30g
- 1 banana
- Frozen Pineapple- ½ cup or 70g
- 1-2 ice cubes

1. Add everything into a blender and blend.

Blend everything together for about 30 seconds, and enjoy!

Breakfast	262
Almond Milk - Vanilla - Unsweetened Almond Milk, 8 oz	30
Kale 1 cup, chopped	33
Pineapple Juice Pineapple Juice, 0.5 cup(s)	59
Banana 1 medium	105
Frozen Pineapple Pineapple, 0.5 cup	35

		Total
■	Carbohydrates (57g)	78%
■	Fat (4g)	14%
■	Protein (5g)	8%

Nutrition Facts

Calories 262

Fat 4g

Saturated fat 0g

Carbohydrates 57g

Fiber 7g

Sugar 34g

Protein 5g

Sodium 209mg

Tropical Lime Smoothie

🍴 SERVES 1

🕐 TOTAL TIME: 5 min

- Coconut water- 1 ¼ cup or 300 ml
- Lime Juice ¼ cup or 60 ml
- Spinach- 1 cup or 28g
- Frozen Pineapple- 1 cup or 140g
- Frozen Mango- 1 cup or 140g

1. Add everything into a blender and blend.

Blend everything together for about 45 seconds, and enjoy!

Breakfast	228
Coconut Water One Coconut Water, 300 ml	56
Lime Juice 4 tbsp	15
Spinach 1 cup	7
Frozen Pineapple Pineapple, 1 cup	70
Mango Frozen, 1 cup (140g)	80

		Total
🟦 Carbohydrates (56g)		84%
⬛ Fat (3g)		11%
🟦 Protein (3g)		5%

Nutrition Facts

Calories 228

Fat 3g

Saturated fat 1g

Carbohydrates 56g

Fiber 8g

Sugar 45g

Protein 3g

Sodium 340mg

Vanilla Orange Smoothie

🍴 SERVES 1

🕐 TOTAL TIME: 5 min

- Almond milk- ½ cup or 120 ml
- Vanilla extract- ¼ teaspoon or 1.2 ml
- 1 medium orange
- ½ of a banana
- Frozen Mango- 1 cup or 140g
- 3-4 ice cubes

1. Add everything into a blender and blend.

Blend everything together for about 30 seconds and enjoy!

Breakfast	227
Almond Milk Almond Breeze Vanilla Milk, 0.5 cup	30
Vanilla Extract Vanilla, 0.25 tsp	2
Orange 1 medium	62
Banna Fruit, 0.5 Banna (118g)	52
Mango Chunks Great Value, 1 cup	80

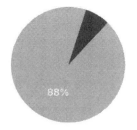

		Total
⬜	Carbohydrates (57g)	88%
⬛	Fat (2g)	7%
⬜	Protein (3g)	5%

Nutrition Facts

Calories 227

Fat 2g

Saturated fat 0g

Carbohydrates 57g

Fiber 7g

Sugar 44g

Protein 3g

Sodium 76mg

Vanilla Protein Smoothie

🍴 SERVES 1

🕐 TOTAL TIME: 5 min

- Milk- 2/3 cup or 155 ml
- Spinach- 1 cup or 28g
- Chia Seeds- 1 teaspoon or 4g
- Vanilla protein powder- 1/2 scoop
- Any frozen tropical fruit mix- 1 cup or 140g

1. Add everything into a blender and blend.
Blend everything together for about 30 seconds and enjoy!

Breakfast	256
2% White Milk Milk, 0.67 Cup	87
Spinach 1 cup	7
Chia seeds 0.33 tbsp	23
Whey Protein Isolate Golden Standard 100%WHEY, 15.5 g	60
Tropical Fruit Mix Tropical Fruit, 1 cups	80

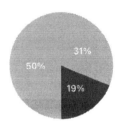

	Total
Carbohydrates (33g)	50%
Fat (5g)	19%
Protein (20g)	31%

Nutrition Facts
Calories 256
Fat 5g
Saturated fat 2g
Carbohydrates 33g
Fiber 5g
Sugar 24g
Protein 20g
Sodium 111mg

Kiwi Protein Smoothie

 SERVES 1

(🕐) TOTAL TIME: 5 min

- Unsweetened almond milk- 1 cup or 240 ml
- Water- ¼ cup or 60 ml
- Spinach- 1 cup or 28g
- 1 banana
- 1 Kiwi
- 1 scoop of vanilla protein powder
- 3-4 ice cubes

1. Add everything into a blender and blend.

Blend everything together for about 30 seconds and enjoy!

Breakfast	304
Spinach 1 cup	7
Banna Fruit, 1 Banna (118g)	105
Medium Kiwi Kiwi, 1 Fruit	42
Whey Protein Isolate Golden Standard 100%WHEY, 31 g	120
Almond Milk - Vanilla - Unsweetened Almond Milk, 8 oz	30

	Total
Carbohydrates (43g)	53%
Fat (4g)	12%
Protein (28g)	35%

Nutrition Facts

Calories 304

Fat 4g

Saturated fat 1g

Carbohydrates 43g

Fiber 7g

Sugar 19g

Protein 28g

Sodium 207mg

Overnight Oatmeal

🍴 SERVES 1

🕐 TOTAL TIME: 5 min

- Rolled Oats- 1/2 cup or 45g
- Milk- 1/2 cup or 120 ml
- Chia Seeds- 1 tablespoon or 10g
- Maple Syrup- 1 tablespoon or 15 ml
- Vanilla Greek Yogurt- 1/4 cup or 60 ml
- Any fresh fruit

1. Add half a cup of rolled oats to a cup or jar.
Preferably rolled oats; they save the best. Make sure the container can hold at least 10 ounces or 300 ml.

2. Add half a cup of milk.

3. Add 1/4 cup of vanilla greek yogurt.

4. Add 1 tablespoon of chia seeds.

5. Add 1 tablespoon of maple syrup.

6. Stir everything together.

7. Add Saran wrap over the container and store overnight.

8. *Optional*
In the morning, top with fresh fruit. Enjoy!

Breakfast	406
Oats Rolled Oats, 0.5 cup	180
Chia seeds 1 tbsp	68
Reduced Fat Milk 2% Great Value, 0.5 cup	60
Maple Syrup 1 tbsp	55
Vanilla Blended Greek Yogurt Chobani Greek Yogurt, 0.25 cup	43

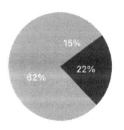

	Total
Carbohydrates (63g)	62%
Fat (9g)	22%
Protein (16g)	15%

Nutrition Facts
Calories 406
Fat 9g
Saturated fat 3g
Carbohydrates 63g
Fiber 8g
Sugar 24g
Protein 16g
Sodium 86mg

Breakfast Burrito

🍴 SERVES 1-2

🕐 TOTAL TIME: 30 min

Burrito

- 2 eggs
- 1-2 pieces of bacon
- 1 large tortilla- 8-10 inches
- Pinch of salt
- Olive oil-1/2 tablespoon or 8 ml
- Cheddar cheese- 1/3 cup or 55g
- Pico de Gallo- 1.5 tablespoons or 10g

Pico de Gallo

- 3 Roma tomatoes (diced) see page 18
- 1/4 of a Red onion (diced) see page 16
- 1 jalapeño
- Pinch of salt

1. Scan to see the whole process.

This recipe was a little more complicated, so I filmed the whole process.

Scan Me

2. Cook the bacon.

Add 1/2 tablespoon of olive oil into a medium preheated pan and throw in the bacon. Cook until desired crispiness.

3. Add the veggies into a bowl.

Dice the tomatoes, onions, and jalapeño, then add them into a bowl. Mix everything together and add in a pinch of salt (this is your Pico de Gallo).

4. Scramble 2 eggs.

5. Assemble the tortilla.

Take your tortilla and add in the cheese and bacon evenly across the tortilla (but don't add food too close to the tortilla edges).

6. Add the eggs and pico in.

Add the eggs in slightly off-center (this will make it easier to wrap the burrito). Then add 1-2 tablespoons or 10g of Pico de Gallo on top.

7. Roll the burrito.

After Adding about two tablespoons of Pico de Gallo in and roll the burrito. Scan the QR code under step 1 to learn how to roll the burrito correctly.

8. Toast the tortilla.

Transfer the wrapped burrito into a preheated pan over medium heat. Put the burrito in with the seam side down so you can seal the seam first. Cook each side of the burrito for 1-2 minutes each until the whole tortilla is lightly brown and crispy. Enjoy! I recommend cutting the burrito in half!

Breakfast Burrito

NUTRITION FACTS

1 Burrito

Calories 610

Fat 38g

Saturated fat 16g

Carbohydrates 37g

Fiber 2g

Sugar 1g

Protein 28g

Sodium 928mg

Breakfast	610
Brown Eggs Cage Free Eggs, 2 each	140
Bacon Bacon, 1 pieces	40
Olive Oil 0.5 tbsp	60
Medium Cheddar Great Value, 37 g	148
Flour Tortillas, Burrito Great Value, 1 tortilla	220
Pico De Gallo 1.5 tbsp(s)	2

If you are enjoying the book, an honest review would be very appreciated!

Scan Me

		Total
▉ Carbohydrates (37g)		25%
▉ Fat (38g)		57%
▉ Protein (28g)		18%

Western Omelette

🕐 TOTAL TIME: 15 min

- 2 eggs
- 1 small slice of ham (20g)
- Diced onion- 1/2 tablespoon or 2g (see page 16)
- Chopped bell pepper- 1/2 tablespoon or 4g (see page 18)
- Mozzarella Cheese (as much as you want)
- Olive oil- 1/2 tablespoon or 8 ml
- Pinch of salt
- Pinch of pepper

1. Cook the ham, bell peppers, and onions.

Add about 1 teaspoon of olive oil into a medium preheated pan, and throw in the onions, bell pepper, and ham. Throw in a pinch of salt and pepper and let them cook for about 5 minutes or until the onions get a slight brownish color to them. Then put everything back into the small bowl.

2. Scramble eggs.

Add about half a tablespoon of olive oil into a low/medium preheated heat pan (try to use an 8-10 inch nonstick pan). Then add the eggs to the pan and throw in a pinch of salt and pepper.

3. Let the eggs sit untouched for 2-3 minutes.

4. Add the ham, onions, bell peppers, and cheese to the omelet.

Lay the ham, onions, bell peppers, and cheese on one side of the omelet. I use mozzarella cheese, but you can use whatever cheese you want.

5. Cover the pan with a lid.

Let the omelet sit covered for about 2 minutes or until the cheese is almost fully melted.

6. Fold the omelet in half.

Take the lid off and fold the omelet in half. Let the folded omelet sit for about 15-20 seconds. Then take the omelet off and enjoy. See the video below if you don't know how to fold an omelet.

Scan Me

Western Omlette

NUTRITION FACTS

Nutrition Facts

Calories 296

Fat 21g

Saturated fat 7g

Carbohydrates 4g

Fiber 1g

Sugar 1g

Protein 21g

Sodium 556mg

Breakfast	296
Brown Eggs Cage Free Eggs, 2 each	140
Onion Onion, 0.5 tbsp(s)	2
Bell Pepper (G) Bell Pepper, 4 g	1
Olive Oil 0.5 tbsp	60
Ham 20 g	54
Mozerella Cheese, 14 gram	40

		Total
	Carbohydrates (4g)	5%
	Fat (21g)	66%
	Protein (21g)	29%

Mushroom Omelette

SERVES 1

TOTAL TIME: 15 min

- 2 eggs
- 1- 2 Baby Bella mushrooms
- Mozzarella cheese (as much as you want)
- Pinch of salt
- Olive oil- 1/2 tablespoon or 8 ml

1. Cook the mushrooms.

Add about 1 teaspoon of olive oil into a low/ medium preheated pan, and then throw in the mushrooms. Let everything cook for 3-4 minutes.

2. Throw in a pinch of salt.

Add a pinch of salt to the mushrooms and let them cook for 1-2 more minutes. Take the mushrooms out and put them aside.

3. Scramble 2 eggs in a separate pan.

Add about half a tablespoon of olive oil into a low/ medium heat pan (try to use an 8-10 inch nonstick pan). Then add in 2 eggs and season with salt and pepper.

4. Let the eggs sit untouched for 2-3 minutes.

5. Add the mushrooms and cheese to the omelet.

Lay the mushrooms and cheese on one side of the omelet. I use mozzarella cheese, but you can use whatever cheese you want.

6. Cover the pan with a lid.

Let the omelet sit covered for about 2 minutes or until the cheese is almost fully melted.

7. Fold the omelet in half.

Take the lid off and fold the omelet in half. Let the folded omelet sit for about 15-20 seconds. Then take the omelet off and enjoy. See the video below if you don't know how to fold an omelet.

Scan Me

Mushroom Omlette

NUTRITION FACTS

Calories 281
Fat 19g
Saturated fat 6g
Carbohydrates 8g
Fiber 4g
Sugar 2g
Protein 19g
Sodium 235mg

Breakfast	**281**
Brown Eggs Cage Free Eggs, 2 each	140
Portobello mushrooms usda, 1.5 mushroom	31
Mozzarella Cheese Cheese, 14 gram	49
Olive Oil 0.5 tbsp	60

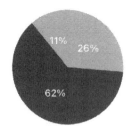

		Total
▨	Carbohydrates (8g)	11%
▨	Fat (19g)	62%
▨	Protein (19g)	26%

Egg Sandwich

🍴 SERVES 1

🕐 TOTAL TIME: 15 min

- English Muffin
- 1 Egg
- 1 slice of bacon
- 1 slice of cheese
- Butter- 1 tablespoon or 15g

1. Cook bacon.

Add a thin layer of butter in a medium preheated pan and fry as much bacon as desired.

2. Toast the English muffin.

Split your English muffin in half and spread a thin layer of butter on the cut side of each half. Put the English muffins on a medium preheated pan (cut-side down). Let it sit for 2-3 minutes or until the edges are golden brown. Then take the muffin off and put it to the side.

3. Fry 1 egg.

Add a little more butter to the same pan you toasted the English Muffin in, then add in one egg. Put a pinch of salt and pepper on the egg and fry for about 30 seconds. Then pop the yolk and flip the egg.

4. Add a slice of cheese on top of the egg.

Add a slice of cheese on top of the egg and let it cook for about 20 more seconds. Now put the egg on the English muffin.

5. Put the sandwich together and enjoy!

Muffin
Bacon
Egg with Cheese on it
Muffin

Egg Sandwhich

NUTRITION FACTS

Calories 422
Fat 26g
Saturated fat 14g
Carbohydrates 27g
Fiber 4g
Sugar 1g
Protein 19g
Sodium 682mg

Breakfast	422
English Muffins 365 Organic Wheat English Muffins, 1 muffin	130
Brown Eggs Cage Free Eggs, 1 each	70
Bacon Bacon - Generic, 1 Slice	42
Cheese Slice Tillamook Cheedar Cheese Slice, 1 slice	80
Butter Organic Butter, 1 tbsp	100

		Total
	Carbohydrates (27g)	26%
	Fat (26g)	56%
	Protein (19g)	18%

Hashbrowns

🍴 SERVES 1

🕐 TOTAL TIME: 10 min

- Frozen Hashbrowns- 1 cup or 70g
- Olive oil- 1 tablespoon or 15 ml
- Salt and pepper to taste

Note: I use frozen hashbrowns. They are very convenient, cheap and easy to make.

1. Cook the hashbrowns and cover the lid.

Add the olive oil to a medium preheated pan. Then add 1 cup of frozen hashbrowns and pack them tightly into a circle. Season with salt and pepper to taste. Then cover the lid and cook the hashbrowns for 5-7 minutes. See video below.

Scan Me

2. Flip the hashbrowns.

Remove the lid and flip the hashbrowns.
Then cover the lid and cook for 3-4 more minutes.

3. Serve and enjoy.

Season with salt and pepper to taste and serve with whatever sides you want.

Breakfast		189
Hash Browns, Shredded		70
Great Value, 1 cup		
Olive Oil		119
1 tbsp		

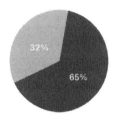

	Total
Carbohydrates (15g)	32%
Fat (13g)	65%
Protein (1g)	3%

Nutrition Facts
Calories 189
Fat 13g
Saturated fat 2g
Carbohydrates 15g
Fiber 1g
Sugar 0g
Protein 1g
Sodium 128mg

Banana Pancakes

🍴 SERVES 2

🕐 TOTAL TIME: 25 min

- 2 Bananas
- 2 eggs
- Cinnamon- 1/4 teaspoon or .5g
- Flour- 2 tablespoons or 20g
- Baking powder- 1 teaspoon or 2g
- Butter- 1 tablespoon or 15g
- Drizzle of maple syrup

1. Mash up the bananas.

REALLY mash them up until they turn into like a mushy banana pudding (I use a fork).

2. Add in the eggs and cinnamon.

Add the eggs and cinnamon into a bowl with the mashed-up bananas and whisk everything together.

3. Add in the flour and baking powder to the mix.

Add the flour and baking powder into the mix and whisk everything together again (this will thicken the batter). Add more flour if you desire thicker batter.

4. Add a small sliver of butter to a medium-preheated pan.

Once you add it in, make sure to spread it around evenly. For each round of pancakes, add another sliver of butter. By the end, you should use about 1 tablespoon of butter.

5. Add the mix to the pan.

Add about 1/3 cup or 80 ml of pancake mix to the pan for each pancake. Spread the mix around a little, and then let it cook for about 5 minutes. Scan the QR code below to see the best way to add to the mix.

Scan Me

6. Flip the pancakes.

Flip the pancakes after about 5-7 minutes or when the edges start browning. Take them off after about 1-2 minutes on the second side. Add some maple syrup, and enjoy!

Banana Pancakes

NUTRITION FACTS

Calories 609

Fat 21g

Saturated fat 10g

Carbohydrates 95g

Fiber 8g

Sugar 56g

Protein 16g

Sodium 620mg

Breakfast	609
Brown Eggs Cage Free Eggs, 2 each	140
Banana 2 medium	210
Baking Flour Bobs Red Mill Baking Flour, 2 tbsp(s)	50
Baking powder 1 tsp	2
Cinnamon 0.25 tsp	2
Butter Unsalted Butter, 1 tbsp	100
Maple Syurp Maple Syurp, 2 tbsp(s)	105

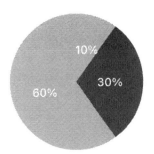

	Total
Carbohydrates (95g)	60%
Fat (21g)	30%
Protein (16g)	10%

French Toast

🍴 SERVES 1

🕐 TOTAL TIME: 15 min

- Bread (preferably Brioche Bread or Texas Toast)
- 2 Eggs
- Milk 1/4 cup or 60 ml
- Organic Butter 1 small sliver per slice
- Sugar 1 teaspoon or 5g
- Cinnamon– 1/4 teaspoon or .5g

1. Bake your bread in the oven at 200°F or 95°C for 10 minutes.

This will dry out the bread. If you don't have an oven, leave the bread out overnight.

2. Add in the eggs, milk, sugar, and cinnamon in a bowl and whisk it all together.

3. Spread a thin layer of butter in a medium preheated pan.

4. Dip both sides of the bread in the batter and add it to the pan.

5. Let it cook for 3-4 minutes.

Flip once the edges of the bread turn golden brown.

6. Flip it and let it cook for 1-2 more minutes.

Take off once the edges turn golden brown.

7. Repeat steps 3-6 as many times as you want.

Breakfast	152
Texas Toast Wonder Bread, 1 slice	90
Butter Organic Butter, 0.33 tbsp	33
Brown Eggs Cage Free Eggs, 0.25 each	18
Reduced Fat Milk 2% Great Value, 0.06 cup	7
Sugar 0.25 tsp	4

	Total
Carbohydrates (19g)	50%
Fat (6g)	36%
Protein (5g)	14%

Nutrition Facts
Calories 152 (per slice)
Fat 6g
Saturated fat 3g
Carbohydrates 19g
Fiber 0g
Sugar 4g
Protein 5g
Sodium 228mg

Yogurt Bowl

 SERVES 1

🕐 TOTAL TIME: 5 min

- Vanilla yogurt (I use vanilla Greek yogurt)- 1 cup or 240 ml
- 1/2 a banana
- 2 strawberries
- A few blueberries
- As much honey as you want
- Granola or mixed nuts- 1-2 tablespoons or about 15g

1. Slice up your banana and strawberries.

2. Add everything to a bowl.
Add the vanilla yogurt into a bowl. Then add in the banana, strawberries, a few blueberries, and as much granola or mixed nuts as you want.

3. Drizzle with a little honey and enjoy!

Breakfast	334
Vanilla Blended Greek Yogurt Chobani Greek Yogurt, 1 cup	173
Banana 0.5 medium	53
Strawberries - Medium Strawberries, 2 only	8
Blueberries 0.1 cup	8
Honey 1 tsp	21
Pumpkin Seed & Flax Granola* Natures Path Organic, 15 gram	71

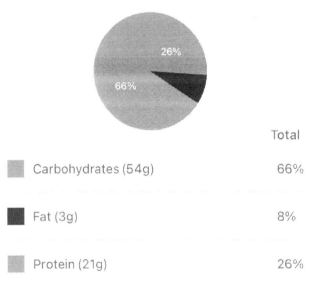

	Total
Carbohydrates (54g)	66%
Fat (3g)	8%
Protein (21g)	26%

Nutrition Facts
Calories 334
Fat 3g
Saturated fat 0g
Carbohydrates 54g
Fiber 4g
Sugar 38g
Protein 21g
Sodium 100mg

Avocado Breakfast Toast

🍴 SERVES 1

🕐 TOTAL TIME: 5 min

- 1/2 of an avocado
- 1 slice of bread
- 1 egg
- Water- 1 cup or 240 ml
- Salt and pepper to taste

1. Toast your bread.

2. Cut the avocado in half, then scoop out one half and mash it up.

Spread the mashed avocado out on the toast.

3. Poach your egg.

Add the water into a bowl, then crack 1 egg into the bowl (make sure to add the water in first). Now throw in a pinch of salt.

4. Microwave the bowl for 1 minute.

See the video below to see what your poached egg should look like.

Scan Me

5. Add the egg to the toast.

Scoop out the egg with a spoon and add it to the toast. Add some salt and pepper and enjoy!

Everything bagel seasoning pairs great with this if you have some!

Breakfast	260
Avocado 0.5 medium	120
Brown Eggs Cage Free Eggs, 1 each	70
Honey Wheat Bread Nature's Own, 1 slice	70

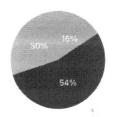

	Total
Carbohydrates (20g)	30%
Fat (16g)	54%
Protein (10g)	16%

Nutrition Facts
Calories 260 (per slice)
Fat 16g
Saturated fat 3g
Carbohydrates 20g
Fiber 5g
Sugar 2g
Protein 10g
Sodium 180mg

Chicken

★ Chicken Stirfry

🍴 SERVES 2-3

🕐 TOTAL TIME: 30 min

- 1 chicken breast
- 3 baby bella mushrooms 52g
- Chopped onions- 3 tablespoons or 28g (see page 17)
- 2 minced garlic cloves (see page 16)
- 1/2 a chili pepper or 15g
- 1/2 a zucchini or 100g
- Spinach- 1 handful or 40g
- Soy Sauce- about 2 teaspoons or 10 ml
- Vinegar- about 1 teaspoon or 5 ml
- Salt and pepper to taste
- Olive oil- 1 tablespoon or 15 ml

1. Dry out the chicken.

Pat the chicken down with a paper towel until dry.

2. Flatten the chicken.

Put the chicken in a big ziplock bag and pound it with a meat mallet or the bottom of a pan. Do this until the chicken is flat. Scan the qr code below to see how I do it.

Scan Me

3. Season the chicken.

Add a generous amount of salt and pepper to both sides of the chicken.

4. Let the chicken sit for 10 minutes.

This will allow the salt to pull the moisture out of the chicken.

5. Cook the chicken.

Add the olive oil to a medium preheated pan, then throw in the chicken. Let it sit for about 6-8 minutes, then flip. Cook the second half for about 3-4 minutes, then take the chicken off the pan.

6. Cut the chicken into slices.

7. Start the veggies.

In the same pan, add in the mushrooms and onions. Cook them for 2-3 minutes, occasionally mixing everything around. Then add in the garlic and chili pepper. Let this cook for about 1-2 minutes, stirring occasionally.

8. Add the zucchini.

Now add in the zucchini and season everything with a little salt. Cook for about 2-3 minutes, occasionally stirring.

9. Add in the spinach.

Next add in the spinach and mix everything around for 15-30 seconds or until the spinach wilts.

10. Add the chicken back in.

After slicing up the chicken, add it back into the bowl. Season the pan with soy sauce and vinegar. Now mix everything together for about 30 seconds. Enjoy!

Nutrition Facts
Calories 411
Fat 19g
Saturated fat 3g
Carbohydrates 25g
Fiber 3g
Sugar 6g
Protein 44g
Sodium 1,408mg

Dinner	411
Chicken Breast mesquite grilled chicken breast, 6 ounces	220
Baby Bella Mushrooms*** 3.3 mushrooms	13
White Onion Onion, 0.2 cup chopped	13
Garlic 2 clove	9
Pepper Red Chili Pepper, 0.5 oz	10
Zucchini 0.5 cup, chopped	11
Spinach, raw, fresh 40 g	9
Soy sauce 0.66 tbsp	6
Vinegar, distilled 0.33 tbsp	1
Olive Oil 1 tbsp	119

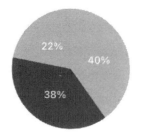

		Total
	Carbohydrates (25g)	22%
	Fat (19g)	38%
	Protein (44g)	40%

Chicken Quesadillas

🍴 SERVES 2-3

🕐 TOTAL TIME: 35 min

Quesadilla

- 1 chicken breast
- 2 tortillas
- Mozzarella cheese- 1 cup or 225g
- Chopped bell peppers- 1/4 cup or 25g (see page 18)
- Diced onions- 1/4 cup or 28g (see page 16)
- Olive oil- 1.5 tablespoons or 23 ml

Seasoning

- Paprika- 1 teaspoon or 4g
- Garlic powder- 1 teaspoon or 4g
- Pinch of salt
- Pinch of pepper

1. Dry out the chicken.

Pat the chicken down with a paper towel until dry.

2. Flatten the chicken.

Put the chicken in a big ziplock bag and pound it with a meat mallet or the bottom of a pan. Do this until the chicken is flat. Scan the qr code below to see how I do it.

Scan Me

3. Season the chicken.

Add the salt, pepper, paprika, and garlic powder to the chicken.

4. Let the chicken sit for 10 minutes.

This will allow the salt to pull the moisture out of the chicken.

5. Cook the chicken.

Add 1 tablespoon of olive oil to a medium preheated pan, then throw in the chicken. Let it sit for about 6-8 minutes, then flip. Cook the second half for about 3-4 minutes, and then take the chicken off the pan.

6. Cut the chicken into small pieces.

7. Cook the bell peppers and onions.

Add a 1/2 tablespoon of olive oil to the same pan you cooked the chicken in. Cook on medium heat for 3-4 minutes (mixing everything up occasionally). Then take the veggies out and put them to the side.

8. Assemble the quesadilla.

Add a tortilla inside the same pan, and add 1/2 a cup of cheese, 1/2 of the chicken breast chicken, 1/2 of the bell peppers, and 1/2 of the onions. Make sure to put everything on 1 side of the tortilla. After adding everything, fold the side with nothing over the side with everything. After you fold the quesadilla, cook each side for 30-60 seconds. Scan the QR code to see how I do it.

Scan Me

9. Repeat step 8 for 2nd quesadilla!

Nutrition Facts
Calories 1,161 (both quesadillas)
Fat 61g
Saturated fat 23g
Carbohydrates 81g
Fiber 3g
Sugar 5g
Protein 76g
Sodium 2,443mg

Dinner	1,161
Chicken Breast mesquite grilled chicken breast, 6 ounces	220
Mozzarella Cheese Kraft, 1 cup	320
Red bell pepper 0.25 cup, sliced	6
Onion 0.25 cup, chopped	16
Olive Oil 1.5 tbsp	179
Flour Tortilla, Burrito Great Value, 2 tortilla	420

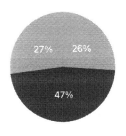

		Total
Carbohydrates (81g)		27%
Fat (61g)		47%
Protein (76g)		26%

Chicken Tacos

🍴 SERVES 1-2

🕐 TOTAL TIME: 25 min

Taco

- 1 chicken thigh
- Chopped lettuce- 1/2 cup or 40g
- 1/2 of a Roma tomato chopped (see page 17)
- Cilantro- 1 teaspoon or .2g
- 2 tortillas
- Olive oil- 1 tablespoon or 15 ml

Chicken seasoning

- A pinch of salt
- A pinch of pepper
- Paprika- 1/4 teaspoon or 1g
- Garlic powder- 1/4 teaspoon of or 1g
- Red pepper flakes- 1/4 teaspoon or .5g

Sauce

- Vanilla yogurt- 1 tablespoon or 15 ml
- Pinch of salt
- Dash of chili powder
- Dash of red pepper flakes
- As much Cholula hot sauce as desired
- Drizzle of honey
- A little lime juice (about a 1/4 of the lime)

This recipe makes 2 tacos. You can use chicken thigh with or without the skin.

1. Dry out the chicken.
Pat the chicken with a paper towel.

2. Cut and season the chicken.
Cut the chicken into thin strips and season with salt, pepper, paprika, garlic powder, and chili flakes. See below how I cut the chicken thigh.

Scan Me

3. Cook the chicken.
In a medium-high preheated pan, add about 1 tablespoon of olive oil. Now, add in the chicken. Once you put the chicken in, let it sit untouched for about 5 minutes. This will give the chicken crispy skin. After 5 minutes, flip each individual piece. Let it cook until you see there is no pink left in the chicken. You will be able to see this since the chicken is cut into thin strips.

4. Make the sauce.
Add the sauce ingredients into a bowl and mix together.

5. Toast each tortilla.

In a separate medium-high preheated pan, toast the tortilla for 10-15 seconds on the first side, then flip and toast for 5-10 seconds on the second side.

6. Assemble the taco.

Add everything to the tortilla in this order:

1. Sauce
2. Chicken
3. Tomatoes
4. Lettuce
5. Cilantro

Enjoy!

Nutrition Facts

Calories 477

Fat 25g

Saturated fat 4g

Carbohydrates 43g

Fiber 1g

Sugar 6g

Protein 14g

Sodium 565mg

Dinner	477
Chicken Thigh Homemade, 1 small	135
Lettuce 0.5 cup, shredded	2
Roma tomato 0.5 tomato	6
Soft Taco Shell Generic Soft Taco Shell one, 2 taco	190
Olive Oil 1 tbsp	119
Yogurt Lowfat Vanilla Activita, 0.5 ounces	11
Honey 0.5 tsp	11
Lime juice - Raw 0.25 lime yields	2

	Total
Carbohydrates (43g)	37%
Fat (25g)	50%
Protein (14g)	13%

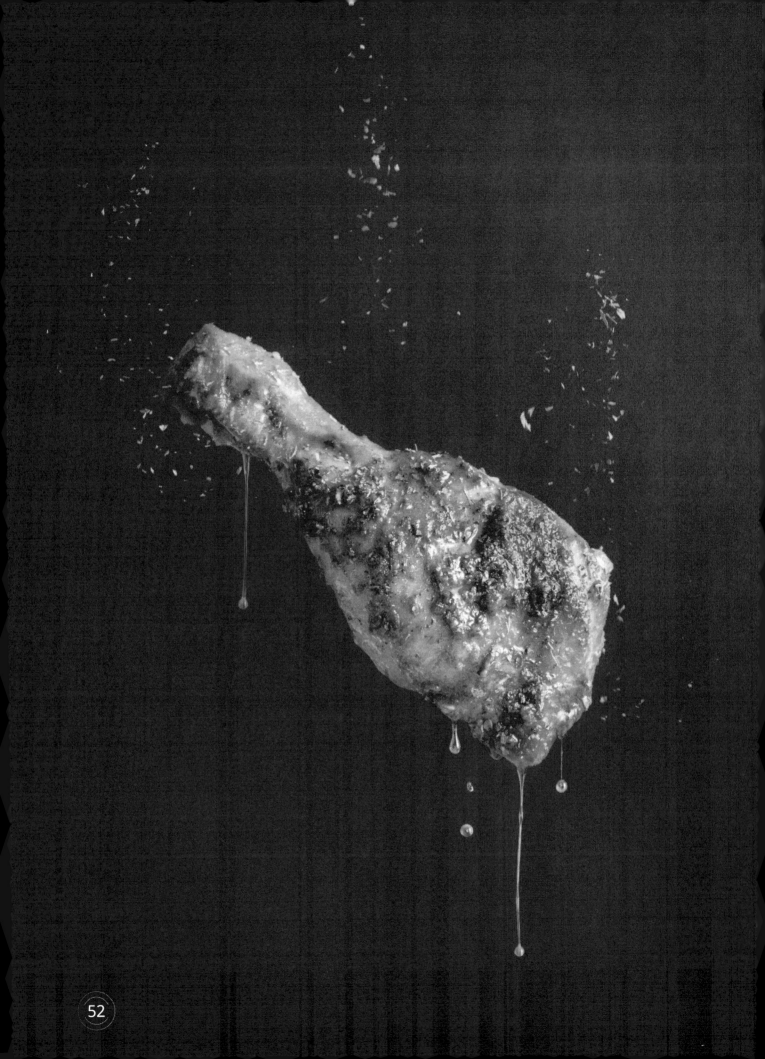

Chicken Drumsticks

🍴 SERVES 5-10

🕐 TOTAL TIME: 50 min

- 10 chicken drumsticks
- Butter- 5 tablespoons or 60g

Seasoning

- Garlic powder- 2 teaspoons or 8g
- Onion powder- 2 teaspoon or 4g
- Paprika- 2 teaspoon or 4g
- Oregano- 1 teaspoon or 1g
- Basil- 1 teaspoon of or 1g
- Thyme- 1 teaspoon or 1.3g
- Cayenne pepper- 1/2 teaspoon or 1.3g
- Salt and pepper to taste

Note: I do 10 drumsticks at a time because they come in packages of 10 at Walmart, so I like to make them all at once. They save very well.

1. Preheat oven to 400°F or 205°C.

2. Mix the spices and seasoning into a small bowl.

3. Season the chicken.
Sprinkle a thin layer of seasoning on your drumsticks.

4. Place half a tablespoon of butter on top of each drumstick.
See the video below if you are confused.

Scan Me

5. Cook the chicken.
Add the drumsticks to the preheated oven and cook for 30-35 minutes. Enjoy!

Chicken Drumsticks

NUTRITION FACTS

Calories 223 (1 drum stick)

Fat 15g

Saturated fat 6g

Carbohydrates 0g

Fiber 0g

Sugar 0g

Protein 19g

Sodium 160mg

Dinner	**223**
Chicken Drumsticks Walmart (Generic), 1 leg	170
Butter Unsalted Butter, 0.5 tbsp	50
Seasoning Chicken bag seasoning, 0.5 tsp(s)	3

		Total
	Carbohydrates (0g)	1%
	Fat (15g)	64%
	Protein (19g)	35%

Honey Garlic Chicken

🍴 SERVES 1

🕐 TOTAL TIME: 30 min

Chicken

- 1 chicken breast
- Salt- 1 teaspoon or 4g
- Pepper- 1/4 teaspoon or .5g
- Corn starch- 2 teaspoons or 6g
- Olive oil- 1 tablespoon or 15 ml
- Butter- 1 tablespoon or 15g
- 2 minced garlic cloves (see page 16)

Sauce

- Honey- 3 tablespoons or 45 ml
- Soy sauce- 1/2 tablespoon or 8 ml
- Apple cider vinegar- 1/2 tablespoon or 8 ml
- Lemon juice- 1/2 tablespoon or 8 ml
- Hot sauce- 1-2 teaspoons or 5-10 ml

1. Make the sauce.

In a small bowl add in all of the sauce ingredients, and mix everything up.

2. Dry out the chicken.

Pat the chicken down with a paper towel.

3. Cut the chicken into cubes.

If you don't know how to cut a chicken breast into cubes, see the video below.

Scan Me

4. Season the chicken with cornstarch, salt, and pepper.

I put the chicken cubes into a bowl and add the salt, pepper, and cornstarch to the bowl. Then, I mix it all up.

5. Cook the chicken.

Add 1 tablespoon of olive oil, then add 1 tablespoon of butter to a medium-high preheated pan. Once the butter melts, add in about half of the chicken cubes. Cook for about 3 minutes on the first side, then turn over the cubes and cook for about 1 minute or until the chicken is fully cooked. You will be able to see once the chicken is fully cooked since they are cubes (don't leave the chicken on for too long, this will dry it out). Once the first batch is done, take it out and put it to the side.

See below how I space out the chicken and flip the cubes.

Scan Me

6. Cook the second batch of chicken.

Add in the second batch, and cook it for 3 minutes on the first side and 1 minute on the second side (or until fully cooked). No need to add any more oil; there will be plenty left over from the first batch.

7. Add in the garlic.

Once the second batch is done cooking, add the first batch back into the pan. Now add in the minced garlic and mix around for 30 seconds while the pan is still on medium-high heat.

8. Add the sauce.

Pour the whole bowl of sauce in, and let it cook for 1-2 minutes (mixing everything around occasionally). The pan should still be on medium-high heat. After 1-2 minutes, turn off the heat, and your chicken is done. Enjoy!

Honey Garlic
Chicken

NUTRITION FACTS

Calories 538

Fat 29g

Saturated fat 10g

Carbohydrates 28g

Fiber 0g

Sugar 17g

Protein 40g

Sodium 1,216mg

Dinner	538
Chicken Breast mesquite grilled chicken breast, 6 ounces	220
Olive Oil 1 tbsp	119
Butter Organic Butter, 1 tbsp	100
Garlic 2 clove	9
Honey Garlic Sauce Diana, 3 Tbsp	90

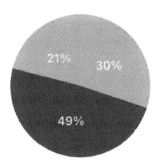

		Total
▨	Carbohydrates (28g)	21%
▨	Fat (29g)	49%
▨	Protein (40g)	30%

Baked Chicken Thigh

🍴 SERVES 1

🕐 TOTAL TIME: 35 min

- 2 chicken thighs
- Olive oil- 1 tablespoon or 15 ml

Seasoning

- Garlic powder- 1 teaspoon or 2g
- Onion powder- 1 teaspoon or 2g
- Italian seasoning- 1 teaspoon or .5g
- Paprika- 1/2 teaspoon or 2g
- Salt- 1/2 teaspoon or 2g
- Pepper- 1/4 teaspoon or .5g

1. Preheat oven to 425°F or 218°C.

2. Make seasoning.

Add all of the spices into a bowl and mix them together.

3. Cut the excess fat off the chicken.

4. Coat chicken in oil.

Add a small coat of olive oil to both sides of the chicken thighs.

5. Season the chicken.

After you add the oil to the chicken, add a light coat of seasoning to both sides and **rub in the seasoning.**

6. Cook the chicken.

Bake the chicken for 20 minutes at 425°F or 218°C and enjoy!

Dinner	409
Chicken Thigh Homemade, 2 small	270
Olive Oil 1 tbsp	119
Seasoning Chicken bag seasoning, 1 tbsp	20

	Total
Carbohydrates (3g)	3%
Fat (30g)	69%
Protein (28g)	28%

Nutrition Facts

Calories 409

Fat 30g

Saturated fat 3g

Carbohydrates 3g

Fiber 0g

Sugar 0g

Protein 28g

Sodium 446mg

Chicken Pot Pie

🍴 SERVES 8-10

🕐 TOTAL TIME: 75 min

- 1 rotisserie chicken
- Chicken stock- 2 cups or 480 ml
- Baby bella mushrooms- 1.5 cups chopped or 135g
- 2 bay leaves
- Diced onions- 1.5 cups or 165g (see page 16)
- Carrots chopped- 1 cup or 140g
- 8 cloves of minced garlic (see page 16)
- Diced ham- 3/4 cup or 90g
- Olive oil- 2 tablespoons or 30 ml
- Butter- 1 tablespoon or 15g
- Salt and pepper to taste
- Flour- 1/2 cup or 80g
- Milk- 1 cup or 240 ml
- Heavy cream- 1 cup or 240 ml
- Frozen peas- 2.5 cups or 285g
- Puff pastry- enough to cover your baking tray

1. Remove all the meat from the rotisserie chicken.

Use your hands or a fork to tear the meat from the chicken. Shred the chicken with your hands or a fork and add the chicken to a bowl.

2. Add the chicken stock to a pot and bring it to a light boil.

Once it comes to a light boil, immediately turn off the heat.

3. Add the mushrooms and bay leaves to the pot.

Cover the pot with a lid and let everything sit for 15-20 minutes without any heat.

4. Remove bay leaves from the pot.

Discard the leaves.

5. Remove the mushrooms and chop them up.

Set them aside for later.

6. Cook the ham.

Add olive oil to a **large** medium-high preheated pan, then throw in the ham and sear until nicely browned (should be 3-5 minutes).

7. Remove ham from the pan and reduce the pan's heat to medium.

Set the ham aside for later.

8. Preheat oven to 400°F or 205°C.

9. Add in the butter and spread it around until it melts.

Use the same pan as the ham.

10. Add the onions, carrots, mushrooms, and garlic cloves to the pan.

Once the butter melts, add in all these veggies. Season with salt and pepper and saute until the veggies become slightly browned and soft.

11. Add in the flour.

After the veggies have become soft, add the flour to the pan and mix for 1 minute.

12. Add the heavy cream, milk, and chicken stock to the pan.

Stir constantly over medium heat until the mix thickens. Should be 2-3 minutes.

`

13. Add in the ham, frozen peas, and shredded chicken.

Add everything and mix until well combined.

14. Add all the ingredients from the pan to a baking dish.

15. Cover the baking dish with puff pastry.

Thaw out the puff pastry in the microwave. Then roll the dough out to 1/4 of an inch thick. Now cover the baking dish filling in the dough. See the video below to see step 15 demonstrated.

Scan Me

16. Bake in the oven at 400°F or 205°C for 20 minutes.

17. Reduce oven to 350°F or 180°C for an additional 20-25 minutes.

18. Let the pie rest for 10-15 minutes Enjoy!

Chicken Pot Pie

NUTRITION FACTS

Calories 2700
Fat 169g
Saturated fat 83g
Carbohydrates 198g
Fiber 27g
Sugar 58g
Protein 100g
Sodium 3,116mg

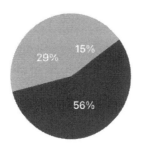

	Total
Carbohydrates (198g)	29%
Fat (169g)	56%
Protein (100g)	15%

Dinner	2,700
Traditional Rotisserie Chicken Walmart, 6 oz	340
chicken stock great value, 2 cup	10
Chopped Baby Bella Mushrooms, 1.5 cup	30
White Onion Onion, 1.5 cup chopped	96
Carrots 1 cup, chopped	52
Garlic 8 clove	36
Diced Ham Kroger, 0.75 cup	90
Olive Oil 2 tbsp	239
Butter Unsalted Butter, 1 tbsp	100
All-purpose flour 0.5 cup	228
Milk D milk, 8 oz.	150
Heavy Cream 1 cup	816
Peas, frozen 2.5 cup	258
Puff Pastry Pastry Chef Puff Pastry From Aldi, 0.5 sheet	256

Seafood

Shrimp Scampi

🍴 SERVES 2-3

🕐 TOTAL TIME: 30 min

- Linguini noodles- 4-6 oz
- 8-10 frozen jumbo shrimp
- Butter- 1 tablespoon or 15g
- Olive oil- 2 tablespoons or 30 ml
- 1 clove of minced garlic (see page 16)
- Red pepper flakes- 1/2 teaspoon or 1g
- Lemon juice from half a lemon
- Chicken broth- 1/4 cup or 60 ml
- Italian seasoning- 1/2 teaspoon or .25g
- Pinch of salt

Optional

- Parmesan cheese

1. Thaw out the frozen shrimp.

Put the frozen shrimp in a bowl and let cold water run over the shrimp for 10 minutes.

2. Boil the noodles.

While waiting, fill a large pot with water and cook the linguini noodles according to package instructions.

3. Add butter, olive oil, garlic, and red pepper flakes to a pan.

In a medium-high preheated pan, add the olive oil first, then the butter. Spread it around until the butter melts. Then add in the minced garlic and red pepper flakes. Stir for 30 seconds to a minute.

4. Cook the shrimp.

Now add in the shrimp, season with a pinch of salt, and let it cook for 1-2 minutes on each side or until the shrimp turn light pink.

5. Add in the lemon juice, chicken broth, and Italian seasoning.

After adding everything in, let it simmer for about 2-3 minutes.

6. Add the pasta to the pan.

Drain the pasta in a colander and add it to the pan. Now turn off the heat to the pan.

7. Mix the pasta in and let it sit for 1-2 minutes.

Top with a little parmesan cheese, and enjoy!

Shrimp Scampi

NUTRITION FACTS

Calories 746

Fat 48g

Saturated fat 11g

Carbohydrates 34g

Fiber 2g

Sugar 1g

Protein 51g

Sodium 575mg

Dinner		746
Linguine	Homemade Linguine Noodles	165
Frozen Jumbo Shrimp	Hannaford, 10 shrimp	220
Olive Oil	2 tbsp	239
Organic Butter	Horizon, 1 tbs	100
Garlic	1 clove	4
Chicken Broth	0.25 cup	12
Lemon juice, raw	0.5 lemon yields	5

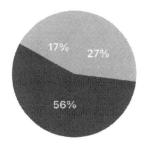

		Total
▨	Carbohydrates (34g)	17%
▨	Fat (48g)	56%
▨	Protein (51g)	27%

Shrimp Cocktail

 SERVES 1

(🕐) TOTAL TIME: 15 min

- Frozen shrimp- 1/2 lb or 225g
- Water- 4 cups or 960 ml
- Juice from half a lemon
- 1 bay leaf
- Black pepper- 1 teaspoon or .5g

Optional

- Cocktail sauce

1. Add the frozen shrimp into a large pot and cover it with cold water.

2. Put the pot on high heat.

Now add in the black pepper, bay leaf, and lemon juice.

3. Keep everything in until the water comes to a rolling boil.

A rolling boil is a point where bubbles rise quickly to the surface of the liquid. Once the pot is at a rolling boil, you want to empty out everything from the pot. See the video below to see what a rolling boil looks like.

Scan Me

4. Empty the pot into a colander and dump the shrimp into a large bowl filled with ice water.

This will stop the cooking process.

5. Add some cocktail sauce and enjoy!

Dinner	128
Frozen Shrimp Frozen Shrimp, 225 gram	117
Lemon juice, raw 0.5 lemon yields	5
Black pepper 1 tsp	6

		Total
▨ Carbohydrates (3g)		9%
▪ Fat (3g)		21%
▨ Protein (22g)		69%

Nutrition Facts

Calories 128
Fat 3g
Saturated fat 0g
Carbohydrates 3g
Fiber 1g
Sugar 1g
Protein 22g
Sodium 1mg

Grilled Salmon

🍴 SERVES 1

🕐 TOTAL TIME: 20 min

- Salmon fillet- 1/2 lb or 225g
- Salt to taste
- Lemon juice from 1/4 of a lemon
- Olive oil- 1/2 a tablespoon or 8 ml

Note: For this recipe, I use salmon fillets with the skin on. I find fillets are easier to prepare and better for single portion sizes. You can also use this same recipe on one large piece of salmon. Just make sure the proportions are correct.

1. Scrape the scales off the skin of the salmon fillet.

2. Score the fish on the skin side.
Scoring the fish means slashing across the skin of the fish. I make 2-3 incisions along the skin. Scoring the fish allows you to cook it evenly. See the video below to see steps 1 and 2 demonstrated.

Scan Me

3. Add a little salt to the flesh side of the fish.

4. Cook the salmon.
Add 1/2 a tablespoon of olive oil to a medium-high preheated pan. Then add the salmon, skin side down. Cook the salmon for about 3-4 minutes or until the skin starts to turn light brown.

5. Cover the pan.
Cover the pan with a lid and **lower the heat to medium**. Let it cook for about 1-2 minutes with the pan on.

6. Flip the salmon.
Take the lid off and flip the salmon. Half of the flesh should be a light pink color. Cook the salmon until you can see the light pink flesh meet in the middle. It should be about 2-3 minutes.

7. Take the salmon off and squeeze some lemon juice on it.
Enjoy!

Grilled Salmon

NUTRITION FACTS

Calories 425

Fat 25g

Saturated fat 6g

Carbohydrates 1g

Fiber 0g

Sugar 0g

Protein 46g

Sodium 94mg

Dinner	425
Lemon juice, raw 0.5 lemon yields	5
Salmon SAMs salmon, 0.5 lb(s)	360
Olive Oil 0.5 tbsp	60

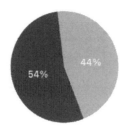

		Total
	Carbohydrates (1g)	2%
	Fat (25g)	54%
	Protein (46g)	44%

 # Baked Salmon

---

🍴 SERVES 1

🕐 TOTAL TIME: 25 min

- Salmon fillet- 1/2 lb or 225g
- Olive oil- 1/2 tablespoon or 8 ml

Seasoning

- Paprika- 1 tablespoon or 12g
- Onion powder- 1/2 tablespoon or 3g
- Garlic powder- 1/2 teaspoon or 2g
- Black pepper- 1/2 teaspoon or 1g
- Salt- 1/2 teaspoon or 2g
- Dried basil- 1/4 teaspoon or .5g
- Oregano- 1/4 teaspoon or .5g
- Thyme- 1/4 teaspoon or .5 g

Note: For this recipe, I use salmon fillets without the skin. I find fillets are easier to prepare and better for single portion sizes. You can also use this same recipe on one large piece of salmon. Just make sure the proportions are correct.

1. Preheat oven to 375°F or 190°C.

2. Mix the seasoning ingredients into a small bowl.

3. Coat the salmon with olive oil.

4. Add a thin layer of seasoning to the salmon.

5. Cook the salmon

Cook in the oven at 375°F or 190°C for 12–15 minutes, depending on the thickness of your fillet.

6. Enjoy!

I like to pair this with the avocado salad found on page **199**.

Dinner	**426**
Salmon SAMs salmon, 0.5 lb(s)	360
Olive Oil 0.5 tbsp	60
Seasoning Salmon grilling rub, 0.62 tsb	6

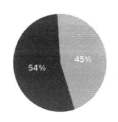

	Total
Carbohydrates (1g)	1%
Fat (25g)	54%
Protein (46g)	45%

Nutrition Facts
Calories 426
Fat 25g
Saturated fat 6g
Carbohydrates 1g
Fiber 0g
Sugar 0g
Protein 46g
Sodium 93mg

Tilapia

🍴 SERVES 2

___

🕐 TOTAL TIME: 20 min

- 2 tilapia fillets- (1/4 lb or 112.g per fillet)
- Juice from half a lemon
- Butter- 1.5 tablespoons or 23g
- 2 cloves of minced garlic (see page 16)
- Paprika- 1 teaspoon or 4g
- Salt and pepper to taste

1. Preheat oven to 400°F or 205°C.

2. Melt the butter in a pan.

3. Place the fish fillets in a baking dish and drizzle melted butter over both sides of the filets.

4. Top the fish with minced garlic.

5. Squeeze half a lemon on top of the fillets.

6. Season both sides of the fillets with salt and pepper.

7. Season one side with paprika.

8. Bake for about 13 minutes at 400°F or 205°C or until the fish is cooked through.

Enjoy!

I only count half of the calories from the butter because half of it will end up at the bottom of the baking tray.

Dinner	290
Paprika Paprika, 4 g	1
Tilapia Tilapia, 8 oz	200
Lemon juice, raw 0.5 lemon yields	5
Butter Organic Butter, 0.75 tbsp	75
Garlic 2 clove	9

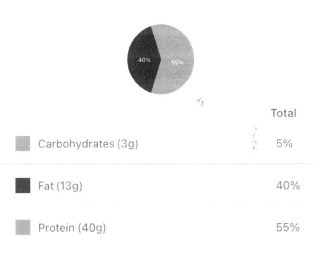

	Total
Carbohydrates (3g)	5%
Fat (13g)	40%
Protein (40g)	55%

Nutrition Facts
Calories 290
Fat 13g
Saturated fat 7g
Carbohydrates 3g
Fiber 1g
Sugar 1g
Protein 40g
Sodium 208mg

Beef and Pork

Lasagna

🍴 SERVES 5-10

🕐 TOTAL TIME: 2 hours

- Olive oil- 1.5 tablespoons or 22 ml
- 1/2 onion diced (see page 16)
- 2 cloves of minced garlic (see page 16)
- 1 box of no-boil lasagna noodles
- Pasta sauce-3 cups or 720 ml
- Water- 1 cup or 240 ml
- Lean ground beef- 1 lb or 455g
- Italian sausage- 1 lb or 4555g

Meat seasoning

- Salt- 1/4 teaspoon or 1g
- Garlic powder- 1/2 teaspoon or 2g
- Onion powder- 1/2 teaspoon or .5g
- Dried oregano- 1/2 teaspoon or 1g
- Red pepper flakes- 1/4 teaspoon or .5g
- Black pepper- 1/2 teaspoon or 1g
- Dried parsley- 1 tablespoon or 1g

Ricotta Cheese mixture

- Mozzarella cheese (shredded)- 1/2 cup or 37g
- Parmesan cheese- 1/4 cup or 25g
- Ricotta cheese (1 container)- 15 oz or 470g
- Dried parsley- 1 tablespoon or 1g
- Pepper to taste
- 1 large egg

Shredded cheese mixture

- Parmesan cheese- 1 cup or 100g
- Mozzarella cheese- 4 cups or 300g

Note: I use the no-boil lasagna noodles, but if you prefer, you can use regular lasagna noodles and just boil them. If I were using regular lasagna noodles, I would boil them after step 6.

1. Mix the meat seasoning ingredients in a bowl.

2. Saute the onion.
Add 1.5 tablespoons of olive oil to a medium-high heat pan. Then saute the onion for 3-4 minutes or until the onion softens and turns a little brown.

3. Add in the garlic.
After sauteing the onions, add the garlic. Mix everything together and cook for about 30 seconds.

4. Add in the ground beef and Italian sausage.
Add it to the same pan as the garlic and onions.

5. Add in the meat seasoning.
Add this in immediately after adding the meat. Cook until fully browned (7-10 mins).

6. Drain out the excess meat grease.
Once the meat is fully cooked, drain out all of the extra meat greases (this is so the grease does not mess up the sauce).

73

7. Add in the pasta sauce and water

After draining the meat, add the pasta sauce and water. Mix everything together, then turn the heat to medium-low.

8. Cover and let the pot simmer on low heat for 20 minutes.

Ricotta cheese mixture

While waiting for the pot to simmer, make your ricotta cheese mixture.

9. Crack and whisk 1 egg in a large bowl.

10. Add the ricotta cheese and mix everything up.

I use the cheese in a container (but you can also use whole cheese).

11. Add in the parsley and pepper with the ricotta cheese mixture.

Add it in and mix everything up.

12. Add in the parmesan and mozzarella cheese.

Mix everything up. Your cheese mixture is done!

13. Preheat oven to 375°F or 190°C.

14. Make the shredded cheese mixture.

In a separate bowl, mix 4 cups of mozzarella cheese and 1 cup of parmesan cheese.

Scan the QR code to see steps 15-28

Scan Me

15. Add a thin layer of meat to the bottom of a baking tray.

I use a 9x13-inch baking tray.

16. Add 3 lasagna noodles over the thin layer of meat.

Just put the last noodle horizontally. Be sure to leave space between noodles as they will expand as they bake. Add 4 if using shorter-sized noodles.

17. Spread half of the ricotta cheese over the noodles.

18. Sprinkle 1/2-3/4 of a cup of the shredded cheese mixture over the ricotta cheese.

19. Add 2 cups of meat and spread it out evenly over the cheese.

20. Add 3 lasagna noodles over the meat.

21. Add the rest of the ricotta cheese.

22. Sprinkle 1/2-3/4 cup of the shredded cheese mix over the ricotta cheese.

23. Add 2 cups of meat and spread evenly.

24. Add 1 more layer of lasagna noodles.

25. Top with the remainder of the meat and cheese.

Spread a thin layer of cheese directly over the noodles. Add the rest of the meat, and then add the rest of the cheese.

26. Cover the baking dish with tin foil.

27. Bake in the oven for 45 minutes.

28. After 45 minutes, remove the tin foil. Then bake for 15 more minutes.

Nutrition Facts

Calories 5,754

Fat 368g

Saturated fat 164g

Carbohydrates 240g

Fiber 26g

Sugar 52g

Protein 387g

Sodium 9,972mg

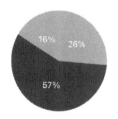

▓ Carbohydrates (240g)	16%
■ Fat (368g)	57%
▓ Protein (387g)	26%

Dinner	**5,754**
White Onion Onion, 0.5 cup chopped	32
Garlic 2 clove	9
Lasagna Noodle (No Boil) Prince, 9 Noodles (2 oz)	630
Pasta sauce Hunts simply pasta sauce, 3 cup	420
Ground Beef Round Beef, 1 lb(s)	960
Ground Italian Sausage Boulder Sausage, 1 lb(s)	1,037
Meatloaf Seasoning Mccormick, 3 tsp	30
Mozzarella Great Value, 0.5 cup	120
Parmesan cheese 0.25 cup	105
Ricotta Cheese The Ricotta Cheese & Factory, 15 oz	780
Parsley, fresh 1 tbsp	1
Brown Eggs Cage Free Eggs, 1 each	70
Parmesan cheese 1 cup	421
Mozzarella Great Value, 4 cup	960
Olive Oil 1.5 tbsp	179

Steak

🍴 SERVES 2-3

🕐 TOTAL TIME: 45 min

- 1 fillet of beef steak, at least 1-inch thick (can be New York Strip, Ribeye, T-bone, or Filet Mignon)
- Olive oil- 2 tablespoons or 30 ml

Seasoning

- Salt- 1/2 teaspoon or 2g
- Black pepper- 1/4 teaspoon or .5g
- Onion powder- 1/4 teaspoon or .25g

Note: There are 3 grades of steak:

- Select
- Choice
- Prime

Make sure to always choose either choice or prime; never choose a select grade of steak. You can tell the grade by the sticker on the package. Look for a sticker like this when picking out your steak. See QR code below.

Scan Me

1. Let the steak sit out for 30 minutes.
Remove any packaging and let it sit out at room temperature.

2. Preheat oven to 375°F or 190°C.

3. Coat both sides of the steak with olive oil.

4. Season the steak.
Combine the seasoning in the bowl and coat both sides of the steak with the mix.

5. Sear the steak.
Preheat a pan on medium-high heat. Then sear each side for 2-3 minutes. If the steak has a side of fat, turn the steak onto its side and render the fat by searing it for 2-3 minutes as well. Don't leave the steak on too long, as you will finish cooking the inside of the steak in the oven. See video below.

Scan Me

6. Add the skillet with the seared steak to the oven.

With the steak still on the skillet, add the skillet to the oven. Leave it in the oven for 5 minutes for medium-rare. A good rule of thumb is 5 minutes in the oven per inch of thickness for medium-rare. Do 6-7 minutes for a well-done steak.

7. Let the steaks sit untouched for 10 minutes. Enjoy!

Nutrition Facts
Calories 1022
Fat 81g
Saturated fat 25g
Carbohydrates 0g
Fiber 0g
Sugar 0g
Protein 69g
Sodium 234mg

Dinner	1,022
New York Strip
Walmart, 12 oz.	780
Olive Oil
1 tbsp	119
Olive Oil
1 tbsp	119
Onion powder
0.25 tsp	2
Black pepper
0.25 tsp, ground	1
Salt
Salt, 0.5 tsp(s)	0

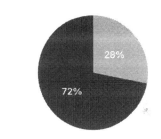

	Total
Carbohydrates (0g)	0%
Fat (81g)	72%
Protein (69g)	28%

Stuffed Bell Peppers

🍴 SERVES 3

🕐 TOTAL TIME: 30 min

- Ground beef- 1/2 lb or 225g
- 3 bell peppers
- Rice- 1/2 cup or 115g
- Tomato sauce- 1 cup or 240 ml
- Water- 15 cups or 3,550 ml

Seasoning

- Onion Powder- 1/2 tablespoon or 3g
- Garlic Powder- 1/2 tablespoon or 4g
- Italian Seasoning- 1/2 tablespoon or 1g
- Salt and pepper to taste

Optional topping

- As much cheese as desired

Scan QR code to see the full process demonstrated

Scan Me

1. Cook the rice according to instructions.

2. Start boiling 15 cups or 3,550 ml of water.

3. Add the ground beef to a skillet and cook on medium heat until fully browned.

It should be about 7-8 minutes. After the meat is fully cooked, remove most of the grease from the skillet.

4. Add the tomato sauce and all of the seasonings to the pan with the beef.

Mix everything together (stirring occasionally) for about 2-3 minutes. The pan should still be on medium heat.

5. Cut out the middle of the bell peppers.

Do this while waiting for step 4 to finish.

6. Add the bell peppers to the boiling water for 5-7 minutes.

7. Add the rice in with the beef.

Put the skillet on low heat, add the cooked rice, then mix everything together until the bell peppers are finished.

8. Take bell peppers out and stuff them with meat, then add cheese on top.

Stuffed Bell Peppers

NUTRITION FACTS

Calories 763	**Dinner**	763
Fat 28g	Ground Beef 0.5 lb(s)	405
Saturated fat 9g	Bell Pepper (G) Bell Pepper, 444 g	96
Carbohydrates 75g	White Rice Generic, 0.5 cup	102
Fiber 11g	Tomato Sauce Prego, 1 cup	140
Sugar 31g	Seasoning mix Generic, 1 Tbsp	20
Protein 55g		
Sodium 1,450mg		

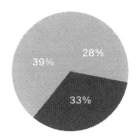

		Total
	Carbohydrates (75g)	39%
	Fat (28g)	33%
	Protein (55g)	28%

Beef and Pasta

🍴 SERVES 2-3

🕐 TOTAL TIME: 45 min

- Ground beef- 1/2 lb or 225g
- Chopped onion- 1/2 cup or 55g (see page 17)
- Minced garlic- 1 clove (see page 16)
- Salt- 1/2 teaspoon or 2g
- Black pepper- 1/4 teaspoon or .5g
- Worcestershire sauce- 1 tablespoon or 15 ml
- Ketchup- 1 tablespoon or 15 ml
- Beef Broth- 2 cups or 480 ml
- Fussili pasta- 6oz or 170g
- Cheddar cheese- 1 cup or 165g
- Milk- 1/4 a cup or 60 ml

1. Cook the beef.

Add the beef, onion, garlic, salt, pepper, worcestershire sauce, and ketchup to a pan and cook on medium heat until the beef turns brown and is fully cooked. Should be about 7-10 minutes.

2. Add in the beef broth and raw pasta.

Simmer on medium heat for 25 minutes with the lid on. At about 12 minutes, take off the lid and mix everything together. Then put the lid back on and let it finish simmering.

3. Add in the cheese and milk.

After you finish simmering everything, add in the cheese and milk, then stir everything up. Your dish is done. Enjoy!

Beef and Pasta

NUTRITION FACTS

Calories 1,456

Fat 55g

Saturated fat 25g

Carbohydrates 144g

Fiber 2g

Sugar 17g

Protein 91g

Sodium 1,402mg

Dinner	1,456
Ground Beef 0.5 lb(s)	405
White Onion Onion, 0.5 cup chopped	32
Garlic 1 clove	4
Worcestershire sauce 1 tbsp	12
Ketchup 1 tbsp	17
Beef Broth Knorr Grandma Beef Broth, 2 cup	20
Fussili Aldi, 170 g	600
Cheddar Cheese Great Value, 1 cup	330
2% Reduced Fat Milk Kirkland Signature, 0.25 cup	35

	Total
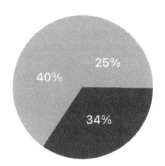 Carbohydrates (144g)	40%
Fat (55g)	34%
Protein (91g)	25%

Chipotle Beef Bowl

🍴 SERVES 1-2

🕐 TOTAL TIME: 30 min

Rice

- Brown rice- 1 cup or 165g

Beef and Brussels

- Ground beef- 1/2 lb or 225g
- Brussels sprouts- 1/4 lb or 112g
- Onion (diced)- 2 tablespoons or 15g (see page 16)
- 1/2 of a medium poblano pepper
- 1 clove of minced garlic (see page 16)
- Red pepper flakes- 1 teaspoon or 2g
- Juice from 1/2 a lime
- Olive oil- 1 tablespoon or 15 ml

Sauce

- Hot sauce of choice- 1 tablespoon or 15 ml
- Apple cider vinegar- 1 teaspoon or 5 ml
- Honey- 4 teaspoons or 20 ml
- Corn starch- 1 teaspoon or 3g

1. Cook the rice according to instructions.

2. Preheat your oven to 400°F or 205°C.

3. Wash and cut all of your vegetables.

4. Season the brussels sprouts.

Cut the brussels sprouts into halves. Place the brussel sprout halves into a large bowl and drizzle ½ tbsp of olive oil over them. Season with salt and pepper to your liking. See the video below to see how to prepare the brussels sprouts.

Scan Me

5. Make the sauce.

Mix the honey, hot sauce, vinegar, and cornstarch together until you get a smooth consistency.

6. Cook the onions and peppers.

In a preheated medium-high heat pan, add ½ tbsp of oil and add the onions, peppers, and red pepper flakes. Cook for 3-5 minutes to brown and soften. After 3-5 minutes, add in the garlic and cook for one more minute. Then take off the heat and put it to the side.

7. Cook your beef.

Add the beef to a medium preheated pan and season with salt and pepper. Cook for 8-10 minutes or until the beef is fully brown. Mix the beef occasionally to make sure it cooks evenly.

8. Add everything in with the beef.

When the beef is about 90% of the way cooked, add the veggies, brussels sprouts, and sauce to the pan. Dump it all in and mix it together. Cook for about 2 minutes, then take the pan off the heat.

9. Mix with rice and serve.

Add the lime juice on top before eating. Enjoy!

Nutrition Facts

Calories 938

Fat 41g

Saturated fat 15g

Carbohydrates 78g

Fiber 8g

Sugar 34g

Protein 66g

Sodium 558mg

Dinner	938
Brown Rice Homemade Brown Rice, 1 Cup Cooked	150
90/10 Beef, 0.5 lb(s)	480
Brussels Sprouts Shaved Brussels Sprouts Trader Joe's, 0.25 lb(s)	47
White Onion Onion, 0.16 cup chopped	10
Chile Pepper Poblano, 0.5 pepper	6
Garlic 1 clove	4
Red pepper flakes 1 tsp	6
Lime juice - Raw 0.5 lime yields	5
Olive Oil 1 tbsp	119
Hot Sauce Sirachi Hot Sauce, 3 tsp	15
Apple cider vinegar 1 tsp	1
Honey 4 tsp	85
Corn starch Corn starch, 0.3 tbsp	9

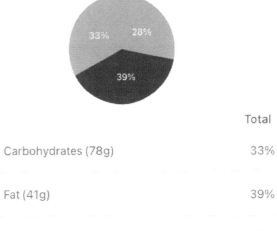

		Total
▩ Carbohydrates (78g)		33%
■ Fat (41g)		39%
▩ Protein (66g)		28%

Pork Stir Fry

🍴 SERVES 2

🕐 TOTAL TIME: 30 min

- 2 boneless pork chops (about 1 inch thick)

Pork Seasoning

- Garlic powder- 1 teaspoon or 4g
- Salt and pepper to taste
- Olive oil- 1 tablespoon or 15 ml

Corn Salsa

- Corn- 1 cob (small kernel) or 60g
- 1/4 of a red onion (sliced) see page 17
- Cherry tomatoes (sliced in half)- 1 cup or 65g
- Spinach- a handful or 35g
- 2 basil leaves
- Red chili flakes- 1/4 teaspoon or .5g
- Olive oil- 1 tablespoon or 15 ml
- Vinegar- 1 teaspoon or 5 ml

1. Slice kernels off the corn.

If you don't know how to prepare corn, see the video below.

Scan Me

2. Slice the red onion.

If you don't know how to slice a red onion, see page 17.

3. Season the pork with salt, pepper, and garlic powder.

Add the seasoning to both sides.

4. Cook the corn.

Throw a pinch of salt in a medium preheated pan. Then add in the corn and just let it sit untouched for 1 minute. Don't add any oil to the pan.

5. Add in the red onions.

Add in the red onions to the pan and let them sit untouched for about 1 minute.

6. Add in the red chili flakes.

Add in the red chili flakes and mix everything up together. Let everything sit for 5 minutes (stirring once or twice).

7. Add in the cherry tomatoes with the corn and onions.

Add 1 tablespoon of olive oil to the pan, then throw in the cherry tomatoes. Mix everything in and let it sit for 1 minute.

8. Add in the spinach, basil leaves, and vinegar.

Turn off the heat and add in the spinach basil leaves and vinegar. Mix everything in and just let it sit for about 1 minute.

9. Cook the pork.

Add in 1 tablespoon of olive oil in a separate medium preheated pan. Then add in the pork. Cook the pork for 5 minutes on the first side, then flip and cook for 4 minutes on the second side.

10. Assemble the dish.

Cut up the pork and add it to the corn salsa. Enjoy!

Nutrition Facts

Calories 658
Fat 37g
Saturated fat 7g
Carbohydrates 35g
Fiber 3g
Sugar 7g
Protein 52g
Sodium 459mg

Lunch	658
Pork Chops Pork, 8 oz	260
Olive Oil 2 tbsp	239
Corn Sweet corn, 1 cob	100
Red onion 0.25 medium	11
Cherry tomatoes 1 cup	27
Spinach, raw, fresh 35 g	8
Basil Leaves Fresh Basil, 2 leaves, 2.5g	0
Vinegar, distilled 1 tsp	1
Garlic powder 1 tsp	10
Red Chili Flakes 0.25 tsp	1

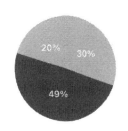

	Total
Carbohydrates (35g)	20%
Fat (37g)	49%
Protein (52g)	30%

Pork Katsu

SERVES 2

🕐 TOTAL TIME: 25 min

- 2 boneless pork chops- (about 1 lb or 455g)
- All-purpose flour- 1 cup or 160g
- 2 eggs
- Water- 1 tablespoon or 15 ml
- Panko bread crumbs- 2 cups or 135g
- Vegetable oil- 2 cups or 480 ml
- Salt to taste

1. Flatten out the pork.

Put the pork between 2 sheets of plastic wrap or in a ziplock bag. Then pound it with a pan or pot. Pound it until it is about 1/2 an inch or 12 mm thick. Scan the code to see step 1 demonstrated.

Scan Me

2. Season both sides of the pork with salt.

Let the pork sit for about 10 minutes.

3. Add the flour to a bowl.

4. Add the eggs and water to another bowl.

Whisk the eggs, then add in the water.

5. Add the breadcrumbs to another bowl.

6. Take 1 pork chop and toss it in the flour.

Make sure to thoroughly coat both sides.

7. Then toss the pork chop in the eggs.

Make sure to thoroughly coat both sides.

8. Then toss the pork chop in the bread crumbs.

Make sure to thoroughly coat both sides.

9. Repeat steps 6-8 for the next pork chop.

10. Prepare the pan.

Add 2 cups of vegetable oil to a pan. Then turn the pan up to medium heat. Try to use a pan that is 10 inches in width or whatever you have that is closest to 10 inches.

11. Cook the pork.

Wait for the oil to start lightly bubbling. Then add in the pork and fry for 4-6 minutes. Flip it over (with tongs) and fry for an additional 3-4 minutes or until crispy golden brown. Remember to lay the pork away from you, so you don't get burned. See the video below to see steps 10-11.

Scan Me

12. Repeat step 11 for the next pork chop.

Note: There is no way to measure exactly how many calories the oil and coating add to the pork chops. That being said, I think this is a pretty accurate measurement of calories and macronutrients.

Nutrition Facts
Calories 671
Fat 40g
Saturated fat 8g
Carbohydrates 27g
Fiber 1g
Sugar 2g
Protein 52g
Sodium 580mg

Lunch	671
Pork Chops Pork, 8 oz	260
Bread Crumbs Italian. Bread Crumbs, 0.1 cup	33
Vegetable oil 1 oz	251
All-purpose flour 0.2 cup	91
Brown Eggs Cage Free Eggs, 0.5 each	35

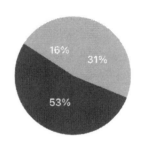

		Total
Carbohydrates (27g)		16%
Fat (40g)		53%
Protein (52g)		31%

Baked Pork Chops

🍴 SERVES 2

🕐 TOTAL TIME: 30 min

- 2 boneless pork chops, 1 inch thick
- Olive oil- 2 tablespoons or 30 ml

Seasoning

- Salt- 1 teaspoon or 4g
- Black pepper- 1/2 teaspoon or 1g
- Paprika- 1 teaspoon or 4g
- Onion powder- 1 teaspoon or 2g

1. Preheat an oven to 400°F or 205°C.

2. Rub both sides of each pork chop with olive oil.

3. Add the seasoning ingredients to a bowl and mix them together.

4. Season the pork.

Add a thin layer of seasoning on both sides of the pork.

5. Cook in the oven for 15-20 minutes.

Use tin foil or a baking sheet to separate the pork chops from the baking pan. Let the pork chops rest for 5 minutes before cutting into them. Enjoy!

Porkchops   280
Boneless Porkchops, 8 oz

Olive Oil   239
2 tbsp

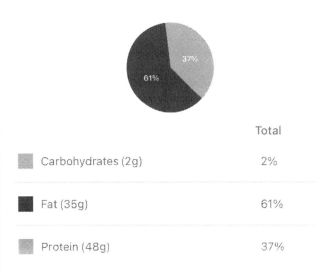

	Total
Carbohydrates (2g)	2%
Fat (35g)	61%
Protein (48g)	37%

Note: Over half of the olive oil gets left at the bottom of the baking tray. So I only count half of it.

Nutrition Facts
Calories 519
Fat 35g
Saturated fat 6g
Carbohydrates 2g
Fiber 0g
Sugar 2g
Protein 48g
Sodium 741mg

Cheesy Meatballs

🍴 SERVES 3-4

🕐 TOTAL TIME: 20 min

Meatballs

- Ground beef- 1/2 lb or 225g
- Italian sausage- 1/2 lb or 225g
- 2 minced garlic cloves (see page 16)
- Parsley- 1/4 cup or 5g
- Parmesan cheese- 1/4 cup or 25g
- Salt- 1/2 teaspoon or 2g
- Pepper- 1/4 of a teaspoon or .5g

Everything else

- Olive oil- 1 tablespoon or 15 ml
- Mozzarella cheese- 1 cup or 75g
- Marinara sauce- 1.5 cups or 360 ml

1. Add all the meatball ingredients into a bowl and mix it up really well.

2. Roll up the meatball mix into balls and put the meatballs on tin foil or a baking sheet.

3. Preheat oven to 425°F or 218°C.

4. Cook the meatballs.

Add 1 tablespoon of olive oil to a pan and cook the meatballs for 5 minutes on the front side and 3-4 minutes on the backside or until fully cooked. You will have to do two batches (make sure to space out the meatballs in the pan).

5. Add 1/2 cup of marinara sauce to the bottom of a baking tray.

Spread out the sauce evenly.

6. Add the meatballs in the tray close together.

Pack them in close, so you can add everything on top later.

7. Add 1 cup of marinara sauce on top of the meatballs.

8. Add 1 cup of cheese on top of everything.

9. Cover the tray with tin foil and bake at 425°F or 218°C for 20 minutes.

Scan the QR code to see steps 5-8 demonstrated.

Cheesy Meatballs

NUTRITION FACTS

Nutrition Facts

Calories 1,781

Fat 133g

Saturated fat 37g

Carbohydrates 34g

Fiber 4g

Sugar 12g

Protein 122g

Sodium 4,177mg

Dinner	1,781
Ground Beef 0.5 lb(s)	405
Italian Sausage Boulder Sausage, 8 oz(s)	517
Garlic 2 clove	9
Parsley, fresh 0.25 cup, chopped	5
Parmesan cheese 0.25 cup	105
Olive Oil 1 tbsp	119
Mozerella cheese shredded Great value, 1 cup	320
Marinara Sauce Rao's Homemade, 1.5 cup	300

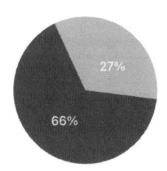

		Total
▨	Carbohydrates (34g)	7%
▧	Fat (133g)	66%
▨	Protein (122g)	27%

White Chili

🕐 TOTAL TIME: 20 min

- Italian sausage- 1 lb or 455g (I use mild Italian sausage)
- Red pepper flakes- 3/4 teaspoon or 1.5g
- 4 cloves of minced garlic (see page 16)
- Water- 1/2 cup or 120 ml
- 2 cans of white beans- 3.5 cups or 700g
- Spinach- 3 cups or 75g
- Canned crushed tomatoes- 2 cups or 580 ml
- Salt to taste

1. Cook the sausage.

In a preheated medium heat **pot**, add the sausage and cook for about 7 minutes or until it turns brown (occasionally mixing it up). Make sure to break the sausage up into little pieces while cooking.

2. Add the red pepper and garlic to the pot.

Stir it together and cook for about 1 minute.

3. Add in the water.

Stir everything together and cook for about 1-2 minutes or until the water is halfway evaporated.

4. Add in the crushed tomatoes and season with salt.

Stir everything up, then let everything simmer on medium heat for 10 minutes.

5. Add in the spinach.

After the pot is done simmering, add in the spinach, and mix everything together. Cook until the spinach is wilted.

6. Add in the beans.

Throw in the beans and stir everything up. Let it sit for about 1-2 more minutes. Your meal is done. Enjoy!

White Chili

NUTRITION FACTS

Calories 1,977

Fat 87g

Saturated fat 29g

Carbohydrates 186g

Fiber 59g

Sugar 17g

Protein 137g

Sodium 6,170mg

Dinner	1,977
Italian Sausage Boulder Sausage, 16 oz(s)	1,034
Garlic 4 clove	18
White Chili Beans White Kidney Beans, 3.5 Cup	700
Spinach, raw, fresh 3 cup	21
Hunt's Crushed Tomatoes 2 cup	180
Red Chili Flakes 0.75 tsp	4

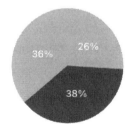

	Total
Carbohydrates (186g)	36%
Fat (87g)	38%
Protein (137g)	26%

Sandwiches

Chicken Katsu Sandwhich

 SERVES 1

🕐 TOTAL TIME: 30 min

- 1 small boneless, skinless chicken breast
- All-purpose flour- 1/2 cup or 80g
- 1 egg
- Water- 1 tablespoon or 15 ml
- Panko bread crumbs- 1/2 cup or 65g
- Vegetable oil- 2 cups or 480 ml
- Salt to taste
- 2 slices of white bread
- Shredded green cabbage- 1/4 cup or 1g

Sauce

- Steak sauce- 2 tablespoons or 30 ml
- Mayonnaise- 2 tablespoons or 30 ml
- Worcestershire sauce- 1 teaspoon or 5 ml

1. Flatten out the chicken.

Put the chicken between 2 sheets of plastic wrap or in a ziplock bag. Then pound it with a pan or pot. Pound it until it is about 1/2 an inch or 12 mm thick. See video below.

Scan Me

2. Season both sides of the chicken with salt.

Let the chicken sit for about 10 minutes.

3. Add the flour to a bowl.

4. Add the eggs and water to another bowl.

Whisk the eggs, then add in the water.

5. Add the breadcrumbs to another bowl.

6. Toss the chicken in the flour.

Make sure to thoroughly coat both sides.

7. Then toss the chicken in the eggs.

Make sure to thoroughly coat both sides.

8. Toss the chicken in the breadcrumbs.

Make sure to thoroughly coat both sides.

9. Prepare the pan.

Add 2 cups of vegetable oil to a pan. Then turn the pan up to medium heat. Try to use a pan that is 10 inches in width or whatever you have that is closest to 10 inches.

10. Cook the chicken.

Wait for the oil to start lightly bubbling. Then add in the chicken and cook for 4-6 minutes before flipping.

11. Flip the chicken.

Now flip it over (with tongs) and fry for 3-4 minutes or until crispy golden brown. Remember to lay the chicken away from you so you don't get burned. See the video below to see steps 9-11. The video is titled pork katsu, but the process is the same with both chicken and pork.

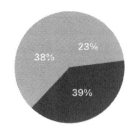

Scan Me

12. Mix the sauce ingredients together in a bowl.

13. Add the sauce to both cut sides of the bread.

Add as much as you want.

14. Build the sandwich.

Top of the sandwich
Bread
Cabbage
Chicken
Bread
Bottom of sandwich

Nutrition Facts
Calories 629
Fat 26
Saturated fat 4g
Carbohydrates 58g
Fiber 2g
Sugar 12g
Protein 36g
Sodium 1,041mg

Lunch	629
Chicken breast, raw, skinless 4 oz	136
Brown Eggs Cage Free Eggs, 0.35 each	24
White bread 2 medium or regular slice	151
Green cabbage 0.25 cup, chopped	6
Katsu Sauce Kikkoman, 2 tbsp	40
Vegetable oil 0.7 oz	176
All-purpose flour 0.16 cup	73
Bread Crumbs Italian. Bread Crumbs, 0.07 cup	23

		Total
▪	Carbohydrates (58g)	38%
▪	Fat (26g)	39%
▪	Protein (36g)	23%

Baloney and Cheese

SERVES 1

TOTAL TIME: 30 min

- 4 slices of baloney
- 2 slices of American cheese
- 1/4 of a yellow onion (sliced) (see page 17)
- 1-2 large tomato slices (see page 18)
- Mustard- 1 tablespoon or 15 ml
- Mayonnaise- 1 tablespoon or 15 ml
- 1 hamburger bun

1. Slice the onion into thin strips (page 17).

2. Slice your tomato (page 18).

Use 1-2 large slices per sandwich.

3. Cook onions.

Cook for about 5 minutes or until softened.

4. *Optional*

Prepare the baloney.

Evenly space out three 1/8 inch cuts around the outside of the baloney (so it doesn't curl up when you cook it).

5. Cook the baloney.

In a separate medium preheated pan, cook the balcony for 2-3 minutes on each side (or until the edges turn golden brown).

6. Toast the bun.

Toast the cut side of each bun on a medium heat pan for 30-60 seconds.

7. Build the sandwich.

Top of the sandwich

Bun

Mustard

Cheese

Baloney

Tomato

Onion

Mayonnaise

Bun

Bottom of the sandwich

8. Melt the cheese.

Add the sandwich to the microwave for 10-15 seconds to melt the cheese.

Baloney and Cheese

NUTRITION FACTS

Calories 675

Fat 47g

Saturated fat 17g

Carbohydrates 35g

Fiber 2g

Sugar 7g

Protein 27g

Sodium 1,212mg

Lunch		675
American cheese	2 slice	154
Yellow onion	0.25 medium	11
Tomatoe Slices	Generic, 2 slices	3
Mustard	1 tbsp	9
Mayonnaise	1 tbsp	94
Baloney	lga baloney, 4 slices	260
Hamburger bun	1 bun	145

		Total
■	Carbohydrates (35g)	21%
■	Fat (47g)	63%
■	Protein (27g)	16%

American Burger

🍴 SERVES 2

🕐 TOTAL TIME: 20 min

- Ground beef- 1 lb or 455g
- Mayonnaise- 1/4 cup or 60 ml
- 1 dill pickle
- 2 slices of American cheese
- 1 hamburger bun

Seasoning

- Soy sauce- 1 tablespoon or 15 ml
- Garlic powder- 1.5 teaspoons or 6g
- Salt and pepper to taste

1. Add the seasoning to the beef.

Put the ground beef into a bowl and add in all of the seasoning ingredients. Then mix everything together (I use my hands).

2. Form the patties.

Separate the beef into 4 balls and flatten them out into circle-shaped patties.

3. Fold each slice of cheese into fourths.

Then stack the folded cheese slices on top of 2 of the patties.

4. Stack the remaining 2 patties on top.

So you should have a sandwich:

Patty

Folded cheese

Patty

5. Carefully seal the edges together so the cheese does not leak out.

6. Cook the patties.

Cook them over medium heat for 3-4 minutes per side or until cooked through on both sides.

7. Toast the bun.

Toast it however you want. You can add it to a toaster or put the bun (cut side down) on the pan for 30 seconds after the patties are done cooking.

8. Build the burger

Top of the burger

Bun

Patty

Pickles

Mayo

Bun

Bottom of the burger

American Burger

NUTRITION FACTS

Calories 1,638

Fat 124g

Saturated fat 42g

Carbohydrates 29g

Fiber 1g

Sugar 6g

Protein 97g

Sodium 2,088mg

Lunch	**1,638**
Ground Beef Round Beef, 1 lb(s)	960
Mayonnaise 0.25 cup	374
Dill Pickle Bicks, 60 g	5
American cheese 2 slice	154
Hamburger bun 1 bun	145

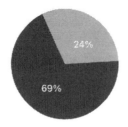

	Total
Carbohydrates (29g)	7%
Fat (124g)	69%
Protein (97g)	24%

Bacon Burger

- Ground beef- 1 lb or 455g
- 4 slices of American cheese
- 4 eggs
- 6 strips of bacon
- Butter- 1 tablespoon or 15g
- 2-3 hamburger buns

Seasoning
- Montreal steak seasoning- 1 tablespoon or 6g

Sauce
- Dill pickle (diced)- 2 tablespoons or 20g
- Mayonnaise- 2 tablespoons or 30 ml
- Ketchup- 1 tablespoon or 15 ml
- Mustard- 2 teaspoons or 10 ml

1. Dice the dill pickle.

2. Make the sauce.
Combine the sauce ingredients in a bowl and mix well.

3. Season the beef.
Combine the Montreal steak seasoning with the beef.

4. Form the beef into 2-3 patties.

5. Cook the patties.
Cook the first side on medium heat for 4-5 minutes.

6. Flip the patties.
When you flip the patties, add 1-2 slices of cheese on top of the cooked side. Then cook for 2-3 minutes on the backside or until fully cooked through.

7. Cook the bacon.
Add a 1/2 tablespoon of butter into a medium preheated pan and throw in the bacon. Cook to desired crispiness.

8. Cook the eggs.
Fry the eggs in a 1/2 tablespoon of butter. Try not to pop the yolk.

9. Toast your buns.
You can toast them in a toaster or add them cut-side down for 30-60 seconds in the same pan you cooked the patties.

10. Add the sauce to the bottom of each bun.
Spread the sauce generously on the cut side of each bun.

11. Build the burger.

Top of the burger

Bun

Fried egg

Bacon

Patty

Bun

Bottom of the burger

Nutrition Facts

Calories 2,531

Fat 170g

Saturated fat 68g

Carbohydrates 92g

Fiber 4g

Sugar 20g

Protein 154g

Sodium 4,343mg

Lunch	2,531
Ground Beef Round Beef, 1 lb(s)	960
American cheese 4 slice	307
Brown Eggs Cage Free Eggs, 4 each	280
Bacon Bacon, 6 pieces	240
Butter, unsalted 1 tbsp	102
Hamburger bun 3 bun	435
Real Mayonnaise Great Value, 2 tbsp.	180
Ketchup 1 tbsp	17
Mustard 2 tsp	6
Dill Pickle 30 gram(s)	4

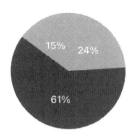

	Total
Carbohydrates (92g)	15%
Fat (170g)	61%
Protein (154g)	24%

PB&J Burger

🍴 SERVES 1

🕐 TOTAL TIME: 20 min

- Ground beef- 1/4 lb or 112g
- Peanut butter- 2 tablespoons or 32g
- Jam (blackberry or raspberry)- 2 tablespoons or 30 ml
- Salt and pepper to taste
- Olive oil- 1 tablespoon or 15 ml
- 1 hamburger bun

1. Season ground beef with salt and pepper.

2. Form the patty.

Form the ground beef into a circle patty.

3. Add olive oil to a medium preheated pan.

4. Cook the patty.

Cook the first side on medium heat for 4-5 minutes.

5. Flip the patty.

Cook the second side for 2-4 minutes or until fully cooked through.

6. Toast the bun.

Toast in a toaster or add the cut side to a medium-high preheated pan for 30-60 seconds.

7. Assemble the burger.

Top of burger

Bun

Jam

Patty

Peanut butter

Bun

Bottom of burger

PB&J Burger

NUTRITION FACTS

Calories 794
Fat 48g
Saturated fat 13g
Carbohydrates 60g
Fiber 3g
Sugar 7g
Protein 33g
Sodium 472mg

Lunch	**794**
Ground Beef Round Beef, 0.25 lb(s)	240
Peanutbutter Jif Creamy Peanutbutter, 2 Tbsp	190
Black berry jam Smucker's, 2 tbsp	100
Olive Oil 1 tbsp	119
Hamburger bun 1 bun	145

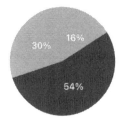

		Total
	Carbohydrates (60g)	30%
	Fat (48g)	54%
	Protein (33g)	16%

Grilled PB&J

🍴 SERVES 1

🕐 TOTAL TIME: 10 min

- 2 slices of bread of your choice
- Peanut butter (as much as you want)
- Jelly (as much as you want)
- Butter– 1/2 tablespoon or 8g

Optional

- Potato chips- as many as you want

1. Cover one slice of bread with peanut butter.

2. Cover the other slice of bread with jelly.

3. Put the two halves together.

4. Add butter to a medium preheated pan.

Spread it around evenly until the butter fully melts.

5. Cook the sandwich.

Cook it just like grilled cheese until both sides are golden brown.

6. *Optional*

Add the potato chips in the center of the sandwich (try it before you judge).

Lunch	442
Bread Organic Bread, 2 slice	200
Peanutbutter Jif Creamy Peanutbutter, 1.5 Tbsp	142
Jelly Raspberry Jelly, 1 tbsp	50
Butter Organic Butter, 0.5 tbsp	50

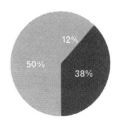

	Total
Carbohydrates (57g)	50%
Fat (19g)	38%
Protein (13g)	12%

Nutrition Facts

Calories 442

Fat 19g

Saturated fat 6g

Carbohydrates 57g

Fiber 8g

Sugar 18g

Protein 13g

Sodium 462mg

Turkey Burger

🕐 TOTAL TIME: 20 min

- 1 hamburger bun

Meat mix

- Ground turkey- 1/4 lb or 112g
- Olive oil- 1/2 tablespoon or 8 ml
- Worcestershire sauce- 1 teaspoon or 5 ml
- Salt and pepper to taste

Optional toppings

- Cheese
- Sliced Red onion (see page 17)
- Sliced Tomato (see page 18)
- Spinach
- Avocado

1. Season the meat.

Mix all the meat ingredients thoroughly in a bowl.

2. Form the meat into a patty.

Make a hole in the middle of the patty with your pinkie finger. This will allow the center of the burger to cook evenly.
See video below.

Scan Me

3. Cook the burger.

Add the patty to a medium-high heat skillet and cook for 6 minutes. Flip, then cook for 4 minutes on the backside.

4. Toast the bun.

Toast the cut side of each bun for 30-60 seconds in the same pan you just used at medium-high heat.

5. Add whatever toppings and serve!

Turkey Burger

NUTRITION FACTS

Calories 486

Fat 25g

Saturated fat 7g

Carbohydrates 18g

Fiber 10g

Sugar 3g

Protein 31g

Sodium 436mg

Dinner	486
1 Hamburger Bun Generic, 1 bun	150
Turkey ground Turkey, 0.25 lb(s)	160
Olive Oil 0.5 tbsp	60
Worcestershire sauce 1 tsp	4
Avocado 0.25 medium	60
Cheddar Cheese applegate cheddar cheese, 0.5 ounce	52

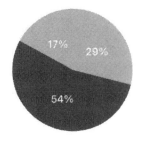

		Total
▨	Carbohydrates (18g)	17%
▨	Fat (25g)	54%
▨	Protein (31g)	29%

Grilled Cubano

🍴 SERVES 4

🕐 TOTAL TIME: 40 min

- Pork tenderloin- 1 lb or 455g
- Store-bought black forest ham slices- 1/2 lb or 225g
- Yellow mustard- 1/3 cup or 80 ml
- 16 slices of Swiss cheese
- 2 large dill pickles (sliced thinly)
- Butter- 4 tablespoons or 120g (1 stick)
- 4 Cuban, Italian, or hoagie type rolls

Pork Seasoning

- Garlic powder- 1/2 teaspoon or 2g
- Salt and pepper to taste

Mojo Sauce

- 2 minced garlic cloves (see page 16)
- Orange Juice- 1/4 cup or 60g
- Juice from 1 lime
- Oregano- 1/4 teaspoon or .25g
- Ground cumin- 1/4 teaspoon or .5g
- Olive oil- 2 tablespoons or 30 ml

1. Preheat oven to 400°F or 205°C

2. Make the sauce.

Mix all of the sauce ingredients together in a bowl.

3. Season pork.

Evenly coat the pork in the pork seasoning.

4. Sear the pork.

Add the butter to a medium-high heat pan and sear the pork on all sides until slightly browned. Don't leave the pork on too long, as you will finish cooking the inside of the pork in the oven.

5. Add the pork to a baking tray.

Line the baking tray with tin foil, then wrap the pork in tin foil.

6. Add the pork to the oven.

Once all sides are seared slightly brown, add the pork to the oven for 13-15 minutes at 400°F or 205°C (this will cook the inside of the pork).

7. Slice each roll in half.

8. Coat the cut side of each roll with the sauce.

9. Toast the roll.

Toast the cut side on a medium-high heat pan for 30-60 seconds.

10. Slice the pork tenderloin.

Cut the pork into thin strips.

11. Build the sandwich.

Top of the sandwich

Bun

2 slices of cheese

Pickles (as much as you want)

Pork (as much as you want)

Ham (as much as you want)

Pickles (as much as you want)

2 slices of cheese

Mustard

Bun

Bottom of the sandwich

Nutrition Facts

Calories 2,428

Fat 106

Saturated fat 50g

Carbohydrates 114g

Fiber 7g

Sugar 23g

Protein 251g

Sodium 6,262mg

Lunch	2,428
Pork Tenderloin Pork, 1 lb(s)	480
Black Forest Ham HEB, 0.5 lb(s)	240
Yellow Mustard 0.33 cup	49
Swiss cheese, reduced fat 16 slice	601
Cuban rolls Walmart, 4 roll	480
Mojo Sauce Wegman's, 4 Tbsp	160
Butter, unsalted 4 tbsp	407
Dill Pickle Bicks, 120 g	10

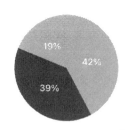

	Total
Carbohydrates (114g)	19%
Fat (106g)	39%
Protein (251g)	42%

Avocado Turkey

🍴 SERVES 4-5

🕐 TOTAL TIME: 10 min

- Sandwich turkey
- 1/2 of a sliced avocado (see page 19)
- Any cheese
- 2 slices of sourdough bread (or anything you have)

1. Toast the bread in a toaster.

2. Cut the avocado into small slices.
See page 19.

3. Assemble the sandwich.

Top of sandwich

Bread

Cheese

Turkey

Avocado

Bread

Bottom of sandwich

Lunch	495
Slow Roasted Turkey Breast Hillshire Farms Naturals, 78 g	75
Avocado 0.5 medium	120
Swiss Cheese Slice Cheese, 1 slice	80
Sourdough bread 2 slice	220

	Total
Carbohydrates (55g)	42%
Fat (20g)	35%
Protein (30g)	23%

Nutrition Facts

Calories 495

Fat 20g

Saturated fat 7g

Carbohydrates 55g

Fiber 7g

Sugar 1g

Protein 30g

Sodium 1,119mg

Sloppy Joe

🍴 SERVES 4

🕐 TOTAL TIME: 35 min

- Ground beef- 1 lb or 455g
- 1/2 of a small onion diced (see page 16)
- 1 bell pepper diced (see page 18)
- 1 garlic clove minced (see page 16)
- 3-4 chipotle peppers minced
- 4 hamburger buns
- Olive oil- 1 tablespoon or 15 ml
- Salt and pepper to taste

Sauce

- Worcestershire sauce- 2 tablespoons or 30g
- Tomato paste- 3/4 cup or 180 ml
- Beer- 1 cup or 240 ml

1. Dice the onion and bell pepper.

See page 16 for onion and 18 for bell pepper.

2. Mince the chipotle peppers and garlic.

See page 16 for garlic.

3. Make the sauce.

Add all of the sauce ingredients to a bowl and mix well.

4. Add olive oil to a medium preheated pan.

5. Cook the bell pepper and onions.

Saute for 3-4 minutes or until the onions become soft.

6. Add in the garlic and chipotle peppers.

Cook for 30-60 seconds, occasionally mixing everything up.

7. Add in the ground beef.

Add the ground beef in with the veggies. Cook until beef is fully browned.

8. Season with salt and pepper.

Season everything in the pan.

9. Add in the sauce.

Mix everything in and let it simmer for 10 minutes on medium-low heat.

10. Toast the bun.

Toast it in a toaster or put the cut side of each bun on a medium-high heat pan for 30-60 seconds.

11. Assemble sandwich.

Top of sandwich

Bun

Sloppy joe mix

Bun

Bottom of sandwich

Sloppy Joe

NUTRITION FACTS

Calories 1,869
Fat 72g
Saturated fat 22g
Carbohydrates 171g
Fiber 17g
Sugar 50g
Protein 125g
Sodium 2,259mg

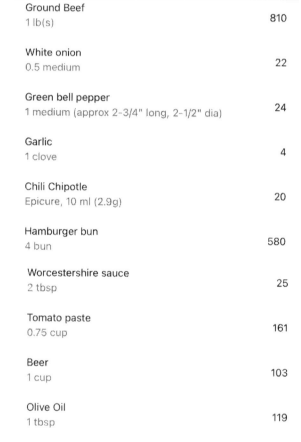

Lunch	1,869
Ground Beef 1 lb(s)	810
White onion 0.5 medium	22
Green bell pepper 1 medium (approx 2-3/4" long, 2-1/2" dia)	24
Garlic 1 clove	4
Chili Chipotle Epicure, 10 ml (2.9g)	20
Hamburger bun 4 bun	580
Worcestershire sauce 2 tbsp	25
Tomato paste 0.75 cup	161
Beer 1 cup	103
Olive Oil 1 tbsp	119

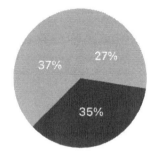

		Total
▨	Carbohydrates (171g)	37%
▨	Fat (72g)	35%
▨	Protein (125g)	27%

Pasta and Meatless Entrees

Veggie Rice Bowl

🍴 SERVES 2-3

🕐 TOTAL TIME: 25 min

Cilantro Lime Rice

- Brown rice- 1 cup or 165g
- 1 bay leaf
- Pinch of salt
- Fresh cilantro- 1 tablespoon or .5g
- Juice from 1 lime

Garlic Beans

- 1/2 can of black or pinto beans- 1 cup or 212g
- 1 garlic clove minced (see page 16)
- Oregano- 1/4 teaspoon or .25g
- Cumin- 1/8 teaspoon or .25g
- dash of chipotle pepper (optional)

Vegetables

- 1 bell pepper (sliced) (see page 18)
- 1/2 red onion (sliced) (see page 17)
- Olive oil- 1/2 tablespoon or 8 ml

Vegetable Seasoning

- Oregano- 1/2 teaspoon or .5g
- Dash of red pepper flakes
- Salt and pepper to taste

1. Cook rice according to package instructions.

Add the salt and bay leaf to the water before it starts to boil.

2. Add the cilantro and lime juice to the rice.

Once the rice is done cooking, add it to a large bowl. Then add the cilantro and lime juice to the bowl and mix everything together.

3. Cook the beans.

Add all of the bean ingredients to a pot and heat over medium heat for 5 minutes (occasionally mixing everything together).

4. Cook the onions.

Add the olive oil to a medium-high preheated pan. Then add in the onions and saute for 3 minutes (occasionally mixing everything together).

5. Add in the bell peppers.

Add the bell peppers with the onions and saute for 5 minutes (stirring occasionally).

6. Add in the vegetable seasoning.

Add in the seasoning with all the veggies. Mix everything up and continue cooking for about 2 minutes or until the veggies start to get soft.

7. Add everything to a bowl and enjoy!

You can add the following toppings
- Guacamole- see page- 193
- Pico de gallo- see page- 34
- Half and half cheese blend of monterey jack and white cheddar (this is what Chipotle uses)
- Shredded lettuce
- Chicken
- Steak

Nutrition Facts

Calories 518

Fat 9g

Saturated fat 1g

Carbohydrates 92g

Fiber 19g

Sugar 12g

Protein 21g

Sodium 928mg

Lunch		518
Brown Rice Homemade Brown Rice, 1 Cup Cooked		150
Cilantro 1 tbsp		0
Lime juice - Raw 1 lime yields		10
Garlic 1 clove		4
Seasoning Chipotle Seasoning, 1 tsp		15
Red Pepper (Bell) Red Pepper (Bell), 1 medium (119 g)		37
Red onion 0.5 medium		22
Black Beans 1 cup		220
Olive Oil 0.5 tbsp		60

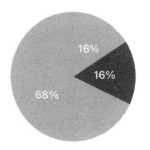

	Total
Carbohydrates (92g)	68%
Fat (9g)	16%
Protein (21g)	16%

Veggie Stir Fry

🍴 SERVES 1-2

🕐 TOTAL TIME: 20 min

- 4 baby bella mushrooms chopped into quarters
- Olive oil- 1 tablespoon or 15 ml
- 1/4 of a red onion (chopped) (see page 17)
- 1.5 bell peppers (roughly chopped) (see page 18)
- Broccoli- 3/4 cup or 55g
- Baby corn- 1/2 cup or 80g

Sauce

- Soy sauce- 2 tablespoons or 45 ml
- Vinegar- 1 teaspoon or 5 ml
- Sesame oil- 1/2 teaspoon or 3 ml

1. Make the sauce.

Add the sauce ingredients into a bowl and mix them together.

2. Saute the onions and bell peppers.

Add olive oil to a medium preheated pan. Then add in the veggies and saute (mixing occasionally) for 4-5 minutes.

3. Add in the mushrooms and broccoli.

Saute with the onions and bell peppers (mixing occasionally) for 2-3 minutes.

4. Add in the baby corn and sauce.

Add it all in and saute (mixing everything occasionally) for another 2-3 minutes. Now serve and enjoy!

Veggie Stir Fry

NUTRITION FACTS

Calories 287

Fat 16g

Saturated fat 2g

Carbohydrates 26g

Fiber 9g

Sugar 11g

Protein 10g

Sodium 2,072mg

Dinner	287
Baby Bella Mushrooms*** 4 mushrooms	16
Red onion 0.25 medium	11
Red belle pepper Generic, 1.5 Medium Pepper	55
Broccoli 0.75 cup, chopped or diced	22
Baby Corn Generic Baby Corn, 0.5 cup	25
Olive Oil 1 tbsp	119
Soy sauce 2 tbsp	17
Sesame oil 0.5 tsp	21
Distilled White Vinegar Great Value, 0.33 tbsp	0

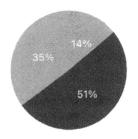

		Total
▨	Carbohydrates (26g)	35%
▨	Fat (16g)	51%
▨	Protein (10g)	14%

Bean Tacos

🍴 SERVES 2

🕐 TOTAL TIME: 20 min

Taco

- Green onions- 1/4 cup or 10g (see page 19)
- Chopped bell peppers- 1/4 cup or 25g (see page 18)
- 1-2 chili peppers (chopped)
- Canned black beans- 1 cup or 190g
- Taco seasoning- 1/2 tablespoon or 5g
- 1-2 crushed walnuts
- Lime juice from half a lime
- 2-4 soft tortillas

Sauce

- Vanilla yogurt- 2 tablespoons or 30 ml
- Cilantro- 1/2 a tablespoon or .5g
- Pinch of salt
- Pinch of pepper
- Lime juice from half a lime

1. Throw the veggies into a pan.

Add some olive oil to a medium-low preheated pan. Throw in the green onions, bell peppers, and chili peppers. Let it cook for 1-2 minutes, occasionally mixing everything up.

2. Add in the beans.

Add in the black beans and let it cook for 2-3 minutes, stirring occasionally.

3. Add in the taco seasoning.

After adding in the seasoning, mix everything up and let it cook for 1-2 minutes.

4. Add in the walnuts and lime juice.

Add in the crushed walnuts and lime juice, then mix everything together and let it cook for 1-2 minutes. Take off the heat and make the sauce.

5. Make the sauce.

Add the vanilla yogurt, cilantro, salt, pepper, and lime juice into a bowl and mix everything up.

6. Toast the tortillas.

Add a tortilla into a separate medium-high preheated pan and let it cook for 15-20 seconds on the first side. Then flip and let it cook for 5-10 seconds on the second side.

7. Assemble the taco.

Start with the sauce, then add in the beans and veggies. This makes anywhere from 2-4 tacos depending on the size of your tortilla.

Bean Tacos

NUTRITION FACTS

Calories 630

Fat 10g

Saturated fat 4g

Carbohydrates 107g

Fiber 13g

Sugar 9g

Protein 18g

Sodium 1,600mg

Dinner	630
Onion Green Veg, 0.25 cup chopped	10
Bell pepper 0.25 cup, chopped	8
Taco seasoning Taco seasoning, 1 tablespoons	10
One Walnut Walnut, 2 Walnut	52
Cilantro 0.5 tbsp	0
Chili Pepper, Green Generic, 1 pepper	18
Probiotics Supplement Vanilla Yogurt Activia, 0.12 cup	16
Black Beans Bush's Best, 1 cup	220
Soft Taco Shell Generic Soft Taco Shell one, 3 taco	285
Lime juice - Raw 1 lime yields	10

	Total
Carbohydrates (107g)	72%
Fat (10g)	15%
Protein (18g)	13%

Fettuccine Alfredo

🍴 SERVES 2-3

🕐 TOTAL TIME: 35 min

- Fettuccine pasta- 1 lb or 450g
- White mushrooms chopped into quarters- 1/2 lb or 225g
- Chopped onion- 1/4 cup or 16g (see page 17)
- 3 cloves of minced garlic (see page 16)
- Half and a half (milk and heavy cream)- 2 cups or 480 ml
- Chopped parsley- 2 tablespoons or 2g
- Salt- 1 tsp or 4g
- Black pepper- 1/4 tsp or .5g
- Olive oil- 1 tablespoon or 15 ml
- Butter- 1 tablespoon or 15g

Note: You can use whatever mushroom you have in the pantry.

1. Cook the fettuccine according to package instructions.

2. Cook the onions.

Add 1 tablespoon of olive oil and 1 tablespoon of butter into a medium preheated pan. Then add in the chopped onion and saute for 3 minutes or until soft and slightly brown.

3. Add in the mushrooms.

Add in the mushrooms with the onions and saute for 5-7 minutes or until soft.

4. Add in the garlic.

Add in the garlic and cook for 30 seconds, mixing everything constantly.

5. Add in the half and half.

Turn up the heat to medium-high and let everything simmer for 8-10 minutes (stirring occasionally).

6. Add in the parsley.

After the pan is done simmering, add in the parsley and season everything with salt and pepper.

7. Add in the cooked pasta.

Add in the cooked pasta and mix everything in. Mix it on the heat for about 1 minute then turn off the heat.

8. Let the pasta sit off the heat for 10-15 minutes.

Serve and enjoy!

If you are enjoying the book, an honest review would be very appreciated!

Scan Me

Note: I do not count all of the half and half toward the calories because over half of it gets dissolved when simmering and a lot of it will be left in the bottom of the pan. So I discarded half of it!

Nutrition Facts

Calories 1,582

Fat 74g

Saturated fat 38g

Carbohydrates 193g

Fiber 15g

Sugar 20g

Protein 44g

Sodium 1,369mg

Dinner	1,582
Fettuccine Barilla, 8 oz	800
Mushrooms, white, raw 0.5 lb(s)	50
White Onion Onion, 0.25 cup chopped	16
Garlic 3 clove	13
Parsley, fresh 2 tbsp	3
Olive Oil 1 tbsp	119
Butter Organic Butter, 1 tbsp	100
Heavy Cream 0.5 cup	408
2% Reduced Fat Milk Kirkland Signature, 0.5 cup	70

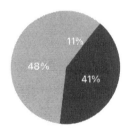

		Total
Carbohydrates (193g)		48%
Fat (74g)		41%
Protein (44g)		11%

Penne Pasta

🍴 SERVES 2-3

🕐 TOTAL TIME: 35 minutes

- Penne pasta- ½ lb or 225g
- Olive oil- 2 tablespoons or 30 ml
- ½ medium onion (diced) (see page 16)
- Red chili flakes- ½ teaspoon or 1g
- 1 clove of minced garlic (see page 16)
- Crushed tomatoes 1.75 cups or 395g
- Salt and pepper to taste
- Pasta water- 1/2 cup or 120 ml

1. Saute the onion.

Add 2 tablespoons of olive oil to a medium preheated pan. Then add in the onion and saute for 5 minutes.

2. Add in the red chili flakes and garlic.

Mix in and cook for 1-2 minutes.

3. Add in the crushed tomatoes.

Stir in the tomatoes and simmer uncovered on medium heat for 20 minutes (stirring occasionally).

4. In the meantime, cook the penne pasta according to the package instructions.

Save a 1/2 cup or 120 ml of pasta water for later.

5. Add the cooked pasta to the sauce.

Drain the cooked pasta and add it to the sauce once it has simmered for 20 minutes. Mix the pasta in with the sauce and add pasta water to thin the sauce (if needed).

6. Season to taste with salt and pepper.

Enjoy!

Penne Pasta

NUTRITION FACTS

Calories 1,219
Fat 31g
Saturated fat 4g
Carbohydrates 204g
Fiber 18g
Sugar 19g
Protein 35g
Sodium 806mg

Lunch	**1,219**
Penne Past Barilla, 225 gram	794
Olive Oil 2 tbsp	239
Onion 0.5 medium	22
Red Chili Flakes 0.5 tsp	3
Garlic 1 clove	4
Hunt's Crushed Tomatoes 1.75 cup	158

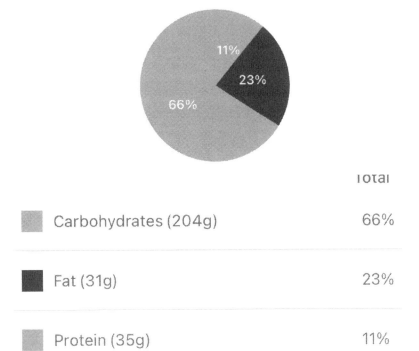

		Total
▉	Carbohydrates (204g)	66%
▉	Fat (31g)	23%
▉	Protein (35g)	11%

Pasta Carbonara

🍴 SERVES 3-4

🕐 TOTAL TIME: 25 minutes

- Spaghetti- 8oz or 225g
- Salt- 1/2 tablespoon or 6g
- Bacon- 1/2 lb or 225g
- Black pepper- 1/4 teaspoon or .5g
- Fresh parsley- 1 tablespoon or 1g
- Pasta water- 3/4 cup or 180 ml
- Parmesan cheese (as much as you want to garnish with)

Sauce
- 2 egg yolks
- 1 whole egg
- Parmesan cheese- 3/4 cups or 75g

1. Cook pasta according to package instructions.
Make sure to season the water with salt before it comes to a boil. Once the pasta is done, reserve .75 cups or 180 ml of pasta water before draining the pasta.

2. Mix the sauce together.
Add the sauce ingredients to the bowl and whisk it all together.

3. Dice your bacon into small cubes.

4. Cook the diced bacon.
Add the bacon to a cold skillet. Then turn the heat up to medium and cook (mixing everything up occasionally) until desired crispiness; it should take 10-12 minutes.

5. Drain the excess bacon grease.
Drain most of the bacon grease, leaving about 1 tablespoon of grease in the pan. Now turn the heat down to low and leave the bacon on the heat. See the video below.

Scan Me

6. Add the pasta, sauce, and pasta water with the bacon.
In a low-heat skillet, add everything and mix it together.

7. Garnish with parsley, parmesan cheese and pepper.
Garnish the dish with as much fresh parsley and parmesan cheese as you want. Serve and enjoy!

129

Pasta Carbonara

NUTRITION FACTS

Calories 1,724

Fat 126g

Saturated fat 46g

Carbohydrates 68g

Fiber 3g

Sugar 3g

Protein 72g

Sodium 2,903mg

Dinner	**1,724**
Spaghetti Cup Spaghetti, 8 fluid ounce	280
Raw Bacon Bacon, 0.5 lb(s)	946
Parsley, fresh 1 tbsp	1
Egg 1 large	72
Egg yolk 2 egg yolk	109
Parmesan cheese 0.75 cup	316

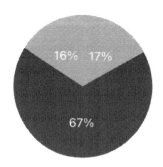

		Total
	Carbohydrates (68g)	16%
	Fat (126g)	67%
	Protein (72g)	17%

Spaghetti

🍴 SERVES 1-2

🕐 TOTAL TIME: 15 min

- Spaghetti noodles- 6 oz or 170g
- Olive oil- 1 tablespoon or 15 ml
- 2 cloves of minced garlic (see page 16)
- Red pepper flakes- 1/4 teaspoon or .5g
- Parsley- 2 tablespoons or 2g
- Pasta water- 1 cup or 240 ml
- Salt to taste

Note: Using high-quality spaghetti noodles will really help this dish since there are so few ingredients.

1. Boil pasta according to package instructions.
Save 1 cup of pasta water.

2. Cook the garlic.
Add 1 tablespoon of olive oil to a medium-high heat pan. Then add in the garlic and cook for about 30 seconds.

3. Add in the red pepper flakes.
After cooking the garlic for 30 seconds, add in the flakes and cook for 15-30 more seconds.

4. Add in the pasta.
Add 1 cup of pasta water to the pan, then add in the pasta. Mix together for 1-2 minutes. Then turn off the heat.

5. Season with salt and add parsley.
Add in the salt and parsley, then mix everything together. Enjoy!

Dinner	735
Spaghetti Noodles Barilla Spaghetti, 6 oz	600
Olive Oil 1 tbsp	119
Garlic 2 clove	9
Red pepper flakes 0.25 tsp	1
Parsley, fresh 0.25 cup, chopped	5

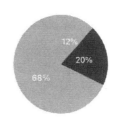

	Total
Carbohydrates (129g)	68%
Fat (16g)	20%
Protein (21g)	12%

Nutrition Facts
Calories 735
Fat 16g
Saturated fat 2g
Carbohydrates 129g
Fiber 7g
Sugar 6g
Protein 21g
Sodium 10mg

Soups and Salads

Chicken Noodle Soup

🍴 SERVES 3-4

🕐 TOTAL TIME: 45 min

- Egg noodles- 6 ounces or 170g
- Chopped parsley- 1.5 tablespoons or 1.5g
- Chicken broth- 6 cups or 1,440 ml

Chicken
- Shredded rotisserie chicken- 1 cup or 120g
- Salt and pepper to taste

Veggies
- Olive oil- 2 tablespoons or 30 ml
- Sliced carrots- 1/2 cup or 75g
- Chopped celery- 1/2 cup or 65g
- 1/2 of a white onion diced (see page 16)
- Ginger (minced)- 1 tablespoon or 6g
- 2 cloves of minced garlic (see page 16)

Seasoning
- Dried thyme- 1/4 teaspoon or .325g
- Dried oregano- 1/4 teaspoon or .25g
- Salt and pepper to taste

1. Remove 1 cup or 120g of flesh from a rotisserie chicken.

I use my hands (it's the easiest way).

2. Shred the chicken up and put it aside.

I shred the chicken with my hands.

3. Saute the onions, celery, and carrots.

Add the olive oil into a large medium preheated pan. Now throw in the onions, celery, and carrots. Then saute on medium heat for 5-7 minutes or until the onions become soft and slightly brown.

4. Add the ginger and garlic with the veggies.

Saute for 2 more minutes, then take the pan off the heat. See how to prepare ginger below.

San Me

5. Add the veggies to a pot.

6. Add chicken broth and seasoning to the pot.

Now bring the pot to a boil.

7. Add in the noodles.

Cook your noodles according to the package instructions. For my noodles, I add them into the boiling broth, then immediately turn down the heat to low and let them simmer for 15-20 minutes (occasionally stirring).

8. Add in the chicken.

Once the noodles are done cooking, add in the chicken and let everything simmer on low heat for 2-3 minutes.

9. Top with fresh parsley, and serve!

Nutrition Facts

Calories 742

Fat 44g

Saturated fat 5g

Carbohydrates 46g

Fiber 6g

Sugar 8g

Protein 38g

Sodium 3,400mg

	Total
Carbohydrates (46g)	25%
Fat (44g)	54%
Protein (38g)	21%

Dinner	742
Noodles Essenhaus, 6 fluid ounce	150
Shredded Chicken Shredded, 120 gram	201
Chicken Broth Great Value, 6 cup	60
Olive Oil 1 tbsp	119
Olive Oil 1 tbsp	119
Carrots 0.5 cup, chopped	26
Celery 0.5 cup, chopped	7
White Onion Onion, 0.5 medium onion	32
Ginger Simply Organic, 3 tsp	15
Garlic 2 clove	9
Parsley, fresh 1.5 tbsp	2
Thyme, fresh 0.25 tsp	0
Oregano 0.25 tsp	1

Black Bean Soup

TOTAL TIME: 40 min

- Vegetable oil (or any neutral oil) - 2 tablespoons or 30 ml
- 1/2 a white onion (diced) (see page 16)
- 1 red bell pepper (diced) (see page 18)
- 5 cloves of minced garlic (see page 16)
- Vegetable broth- 4 cups or 960 ml
- 3 cans of black beans- 45 oz or 1.33 L
- 1 can of fire-roasted diced tomatoes- 14oz or 400g
- Canned green chilis- 1/2 cup or 115g
- Hot sauce- 1 tablespoon or 15 ml
- Salt- 1/2 teaspoon or 2g
- Juice from 2 limes

Spices
- Chili powder- 1 teaspoon or 2g
- Ground cumin- 1 teaspoon or 2g
- Paprika- 1 teaspoon or 2g

Optional toppings
- Tortilla strips or tortilla chips
- Sliced avocado
- Cheese
- Fresh cilantro

1. Cook the onions and bell peppers.
Add vegetable oil to a large **POT** that is preheated on medium heat. Then add in the onions and bell peppers and saute for 5-7 minutes (or until the veggies get soft and have a little color to them).

2. Add in the garlic and spices.
Add in the garlic and spices and saute for 60 seconds (occasionally stirring everything up).

3. Add in the broth, black beans, tomatoes, green chiles, and salt
Add everything in the pot with the onions and bell peppers and let it simmer for 5 minutes (occasionally stirring everything). Then take the soup off of the heat.

4. Pour half of the soup into a blender.
Blend soup for 30-60 seconds or until smooth.

5. Add the blended soup back into the pot with the rest of the soup.
Mix it all up.

6. Add the lime juice and hot sauce.
Top with whatever toppings and serve Enjoy!

Black Bean Soup

NUTRITION FACTS

Calories 1,682

Fat 28g

Saturated fat 4g

Carbohydrates 271g

Fiber 59g

Sugar 39g

Protein 69g

Sodium 7,964mg

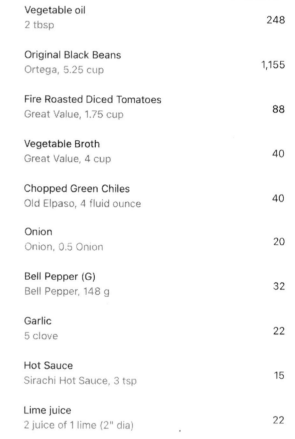

Dinner	1,682
Vegetable oil 2 tbsp	248
Original Black Beans Ortega, 5.25 cup	1,155
Fire Roasted Diced Tomatoes Great Value, 1.75 cup	88
Vegetable Broth Great Value, 4 cup	40
Chopped Green Chiles Old Elpaso, 4 fluid ounce	40
Onion Onion, 0.5 Onion	20
Bell Pepper (G) Bell Pepper, 148 g	32
Garlic 5 clove	22
Hot Sauce Sirachi Hot Sauce, 3 tsp	15
Lime juice 2 juice of 1 lime (2" dia)	22

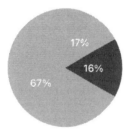

	Total
Carbohydrates (271g)	67%
Fat (28g)	16%
Protein (69g)	17%

Spicy Corn Soup

🍴 SERVES 1-2

🕐 TOTAL TIME: 30 minutes

- 1/2 an onion (diced) (see page 16)
- 1/2 a jalapeño (chopped)
- Butter- 2 tablespoons or 30g
- 3 cloves of minced garlic (see page 16)
- Chicken stock- 2 cups or 480 ml
- Frozen corn kernels- 3 cups or 510g
- Sugar- 1/2 tablespoon or 7g
- Salt- 1 teaspoon or 4g
- Half and half (heavy cream and milk)- 3/4 cup or 180 ml
- Fresh cilantro- 1/2 cup or 4g

Powders

- Flour- 1.5 tablespoons or 15g
- Ground cumin- 1 teaspoon or 2g
- Chili powder- 1/2 teaspoon or 1g

Optional Toppings

- Bacon (crumbled)
- Parmesan cheese
- Sliced Jalapeño

1. Saute the onion and jalapeño.

Add 2 tablespoons of butter to a large **pot** over medium heat and melt it.

Then add in the onion and jalapeño. Saute for 5-7 minutes (occasionally stirring everything up) or until the onions turn soft and slightly brown.

2. Add in the garlic.

Once the onions are soft, stir in the garlic and cook for an additional 30-60 seconds.

3. Add in the powders.

Mix in and cook for 2 minutes.

4. Add in the chicken stock.

Turn the heat to high and bring the pot to a boil.

5. Add in the corn kernels, salt, and sugar.

Once the broth has come to a light boil, immediately add in the frozen corn kernels (This will cause the boil to cease for a little). After adding in the kernels, season with salt and sugar.

6. Reduce the heat to low.

Once the pot comes to a boil again, reduce the heat to low. See the video below to see steps 5-6.

Scan Me

7. Let the pot simmer for 10 minutes.

8. Add in half and half and cilantro.

After the pot is done simmering add in the half and half and cilantro. Turn off the heat and mix it all in.

9. Serve!

You can serve as is or add some of the optional toppings. Enjoy!

Nutrition Facts
Calories 1,036
Fat 47g
Saturated fat 27g
Carbohydrates 132g
Fiber 7g
Sugar 40g
Protein 28g
Sodium 407mg

Lunch	1,036
White Onion Onion, 0.5 cup chopped	32
Jalapeño 0.5 whole	3
Butter Organic Butter, 2 tbsp	200
Garlic 3 clove	13
Stock, Unsalted Chicken College Inn, 2 cup	20
Frozen Corn Great Value, 3 cup	450
Sugar 0.5 tbsp	24
Half and half 0.75 cup	236
Cilantro 0.5 cup	2
All-purpose flour 1.5 tbsp	43
Cumin, ground 1 tsp	10
Chili powder 0.5 tsp	4

	Total
Carbohydrates (132g)	49%
Fat (47g)	40%
Protein (28g)	11%

Cilantro Ranch Pasta Salad

🍴 SERVES 1-2

🕐 TOTAL TIME: 20 minutes

- Bow tie pasta- 1/4 lb or 112g

Toppings

- Cherry tomatoes cut in half - 1/3 cup or 55g
- Cheddar cheese (cubed or shredded)- 1/3 cup or 55g
- 1/4 of an English cucumber (diced)
- 1/8 of a red onion (diced) (see page 16)
- 1 slice of cooked bacon crumbled

Dressing

- Green salsa- 1/2 cup or 120 ml
- Mayonnaise- 1/4 cup or 60 ml
- Cilantro- 1/3 cup or 3g
- Lime juice- 1 tablespoon or 15 ml
- Garlic powder- 1 teaspoon or 4g
- Onion powder- 1 teaspoon or 2g
- Salt- 1/2 teaspoon or 2g
- Black pepper- 1/4 teaspoon or .5g

1. Cook pasta according to package instructions.

2. Combine the pasta and dressing ingredients into a bowl.

Mix everything together.

3. Add the toppings to the bowl.

Mix together and enjoy!

Cilantro Ranch Pasta Salad

NUTRITION FACTS

Calories 1,203
Fat 77g
Saturated fat 19g
Carbohydrates 102g
Fiber 6g
Sugar 11g
Protein 29g
Sodium 1,832mg

Lunch	1,203
Pasta Bow tie pasta, 0.25 lb(s)	400
Cherry tomatoes 0.33 cup	9
Cheddar cheese 0.33 cup, diced	178
English cucumber 0.25 regular	8
Red onion 0.12 medium	6
Bacon Bacon - Generic, 1 Slice	42
Roasted Poblano Salsa Cremosa Herdez, 110 g	177
Real Mayonnaise Great Value, 4 tbsp.	360
Cilantro 0.33 cup	1
Lime juice 3 tsp	4
Garlic powder 1 tsp	10
Onion powder 1 tsp	8

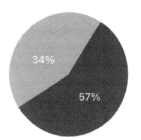

		Total
	Carbohydrates (102g)	34%
	Fat (77g)	57%
	Protein (29g)	9%

Chicken Curry Lettuce Wrap

🍴 SERVES 2-3

🕐 TOTAL TIME: 4 hours

- Rotisserie chicken- 1/2 lb or 225g
- Celery (chopped)- 1/2 cup or 65g
- 1/2 an apple diced (into half-inch cubes)
- Raisins- 2 tablespoons or 17g
- Sliced almonds- 2 tablespoons or 12g
- Green onions (chopped)- 2 tablespoons or 8g (see page 19)
- Lettuce leaves (as many as you want)

Sauce

- Mayonnaise- .375 cup or 90 ml
- Curry powder- 1/2 tablespoon or 3.5g
- Lemon juice- 1/2 teaspoon or 2.5 ml
- Garlic powder- 1/8 teaspoon or .5g
- Salt and pepper to taste

Note: I buy sliced almonds instead of slicing them myself. If you only have regular almonds, just chop them in half or fourths before toasting.

1. Remove flesh from rotisserie chicken.

I use my hands.

2. Shred the chicken.

Shred rotisserie chicken with a fork or your hands.

3. Roast the almonds.

Add the almond slices into a medium preheated pan. Let them cook for 3-4 minutes (occasionally stirring everything up) or until the almonds get a little color to them.

4. Mix everything up.

Add the chicken, celery, apple, raisins, green onions, and almonds into a bowl and mix them together.

5. Make the sauce.

Add the sauce ingredients to a bowl and mix thoroughly.

6. Mix everything.

Add the sauce to the bowl with the rest of the ingredients. Mix everything thoroughly.

7. Chill in the fridge for 3-4 hours.

8. Serve in a lettuce wrap.

This salad is much better when served in a lettuce wrap. Just add some of the salad on a lettuce leaf.

Chicken Curry Lettuce Wrap

NUTRITION FACTS

Calories 1,284

Fat 98g

Saturated fat 19g

Carbohydrates 37g

Fiber 6g

Sugar 28g

Protein 45g

Sodium 674mg

Dinner	**1,284**
Rotisserie Chicken Rotisserie chicken, 0.5 lb(s)	453
Celery 0.5 cup, chopped	7
Apple 0.5 medium	52
Raisins 2 tbsp(s)	60
Almonds 2 tbsp(s)	99
Green onions 2 tbsp, chopped	4
Iceberg Lettuce Leaves 1 cup, chopped	8
Mayonnaise Hellman's Mayonnaise, 0.38 cup(s)	600
Lemon juice, raw 0.5 tsp(s)	1

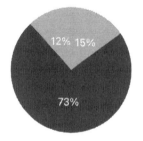

	Total
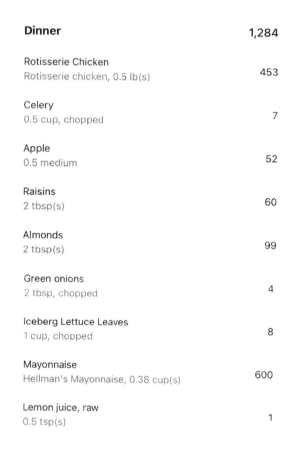 Carbohydrates (37g)	12%
Fat (98g)	73%
Protein (45g)	15%

Sweet and Tangy Kale Salad

🍴 SERVES 1-2

🕐 TOTAL TIME: 10 minutes

- Kale- 3 cups or 90g
- 1 apple chopped into small cubes
- Craisins- 1/3 cup or 45g
- Sliced almonds- 1/2 cup or 48g
- Feta cheese- 1/2 cup or 70g

Dressing
- Olive oil- 1/4 cup or 60 ml
- Juice from 1 lemon
- White wine vinegar- 1 teaspoon or 5 ml
- Lemon zest- 1/2 teaspoon or 1g
- 1 clove of minced garlic (see page 16)
- Sugar- 1 teaspoon or 5g
- Salt- 1/2 teaspoon or 2g
- Pepper- 1/2 teaspoon or 1g

1. Make the dressing.
Combine the dressing ingredients in a bowl and whisk together.

2. Combine the salad ingredients in a large bowl.

3. Add the dressing to the bowl.

4. Mix everything together.
Enjoy!

Sweet and Tangy Kale Salad

NUTRITION FACTS

Calories 1,010

Fat 72g

Saturated fat 16g

Carbohydrates 77g

Fiber 12g

Sugar 57g

Protein 20g

Sodium 2,046mg

Lunch	**1,010**
Kale, raw 3 cup, chopped	26
Apple 1 medium	95
Craisins Craisins, 0.33 cup	130
Almonds Whole almonds, 0.5 cup	80
Feta Cheese Odyssey Feta Cheese, 70 gram	173
Olive Oil 4 tbsp	477
Lemon juice, raw 1 lemon yields	10
Gourmet White Wine Vinegar Pompeian, 0.33 tbsp	0
Lemon Lemon Zest, 0.15 Tbsp	0
Sugar 1 tsp	16
Garlic Clove ~ 4g per average clove Fresh, 1 clove	4

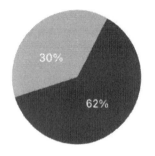

	Total
Carbohydrates (77g)	30%
Fat (72g)	62%
Protein (20g)	8%

Greek Salad

TOTAL TIME: 10 minutes

- 1 English cucumber (diced)
- Cherry tomatoes (sliced in half)- 2 cups or 330g
- 1/2 a red onion (sliced or diced) (see page 16)
- Kalamata olives (pitted)- 1/2 cup or 70g
- Feta cheese- 1 cup or 140g

Dressing

- Extra virgin olive oil- 1/4 cup or 60 ml
- Lemon Juice- 1/4 cup or 60 ml
- Red wine vinegar- 2 tablespoons or 30 ml
- Oregano- 1/2 teaspoon or .5g
- Salt and pepper to taste

1. Make the dressing.

Combine the dressing ingredients in a bowl and whisk together.

2. Combine the salad ingredients in a large bowl.

3. Add the dressing to the bowl.

4. Mix everything together.

Enjoy!

Greek Salad

NUTRITION FACTS

Calories 1,201

Fat 106g

Saturated fat 32g

Carbohydrates 30g

Fiber 6g

Sugar 15g

Protein 28g

Sodium 2,664mg

Dinner	1,201
English cucumber 1 regular	30
Cherry Tomato Organic, 2 cup (149g)	54
Red onion 0.5 medium	22
Sliced Kalamata Olives Great Value, 8 tbsp.	240
Crumbled Feta Giant Natural Feta Cheese Crumbled, 1 cup	360
Olive Oil 4 tbsp	477
Lemon juice, raw 1 lemon yields	10
Vinegar, red wine 2 tbsp	6
Oregano 0.5 tsp	2

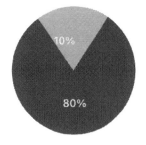

	Total
Carbohydrates (30g)	10%
Fat (106g)	80%
Protein (28g)	9%

Potato Salad

🍴 SERVES 3-4

🕐 TOTAL TIME: 12 hours

- Frozen diced potatoes- 1 lb or 455g
- Water- 2 tablespoons or 30 ml
- Paprika- 1 teaspoon or 2g

Potato seasoning

- Apple cider vinegar- 1 tablespoon or 15 ml
- Yellow mustard- 1/2 tablespoon or 8 ml
- Salt- 3/4 teaspoon or 3g
- Pepper 1/8 teaspoon or .25g

Salad sauce

- Mayonnaise- 1 cup or 240 ml
- 2 hard-boiled eggs (chopped)
- Celery (chopped)- 1/2 cup or 65g
- Diced Onion- 2 tablespoons or 8g (see page 16)

Night before ...

1. Prep the potatoes.

Add the frozen potatoes to a large bowl and pour the water on them.

2. Cook the potatoes.

Cover the bowl with plastic wrap or tin foil, Then microwave for 15-20 minutes (or until the potatoes are completely thawed out and cooked). At the halfway point, take the potatoes out and stir them up.

Note: Microwave time will vary depending on microwave power and thickness of the potatoes (so you might need to experiment a little).

3. Make the seasoning.

Add the seasoning ingredients to a bowl and whisk together.

4. Add the potato seasoning to the potatoes.

Add the seasoning to the bowl and mix everything up.

5. Cover the bowl in plastic wrap and leave the bowl in the fridge overnight.

6. Boil water.

Bring a pot of water to a boil (add enough water to cover 2 eggs in about an inch of water).

7. Add in the eggs.

Turn the heat down to low right before adding in your eggs (this way, they don't crack when you add them in).

8. Boil the eggs for 13-14 minutes.

After adding the eggs, immediately turn the heat back up and boil for 13-14 minutes.

9. Peel the eggshells.

Run water over the eggs as you peel off the eggshells.

10. Chop the eggs into little pieces.

11. Make the salad sauce.

Add all of the salad sauce ingredients to a bowl and mix thoroughly.

12. Refrigerate overnight.

Add the plastic wrap to the bowl and refrigerate.

Day of.....

13. Mix the salad mix and potato mix together.

Mix everything thoroughly.

14. Top with paprika and serve.

Enjoy!

Dinner	2,014
Diced Potatoes Simply Potatoes, 1 lb(s)	355
Apple cider vinegar 3 tsp	3
Mustard 0.5 tbsp	5
Mayonnaise 1 cup	1,496
Brown Eggs Cage Free Eggs, 2 each	140
Celery 0.5 cup, chopped	7
Onion 2 tbsp, chopped	8

	Total
Carbohydrates (90g)	17%
Fat (174g)	78%
Protein (22g)	5%

Nutrition Facts
Calories 2,014
Fat 174g
Saturated fat 29g
Carbohydrates 90g
Fiber 9g
Sugar 3g
Protein 22g
Sodium 1,928mg

Snacks

Bruschetta

🍴 SERVES 1

🕐 TOTAL TIME: 10 min

- 1 slice of sourdough bread

Toppings

- 1 roma tomato diced (see page 17)
- Chopped basil leaves- 1 tablespoon or 3g
- 1 minced garlic clove (see page 16)
- Olive oil- 1 tablespoon or 15 ml

1. Add the tomatoes and basil leaves into a bowl.

Add them into a bowl, season with salt and pepper, then drizzle about 1 teaspoon of olive oil in the bowl. Now mix everything up.

2. Cook the garlic clove.

Add 1 teaspoon of olive oil to a medium-high preheated pan and cook the garlic for 1 minute. Then add it to the bowl and mix in.

3. Toast the bread.

In the same pan as the garlic add another teaspoon of olive oil. Then toast each side of the bread for about 1-2 minutes or until each side turns golden brown.

4. Add the toppings to the bread.

Add all of the toppings to the bread and drizzle some olive oil over everything. Enjoy!

Snacks	266
Bread, Sourdough Pepperidge Farm, 1 slice	130
Roma tomato 1 tomato	11
Basil Leaves Fresh Basil, 6.25 leaves, 2.5g	1
Garlic 1 clove	4
Olive Oil 1 tbsp	119

	Total
Carbohydrates (28g)	42%
Fat (15g)	50%
Protein (4g)	8%

Nutrition Facts
Calories 266
Fat 15g
Saturated fat 2g
Carbohydrates 28g
Fiber 1g
Sugar 4g
Protein 4g
Sodium 234mg

Cottage Cheese Bowl

🍴 SERVES 1

🕐 TOTAL TIME: 5 min

- Cottage cheese- 1/2 cup or 135g
- Blueberries- 1/2 cup or 70g
- 1/4 teaspoon of nutmeg or .5g
- Maple Syrup (as much as you want)

Note: I recommend eating this as a late-night snack. Cottage cheese is full of casein protein, which is great to eat right before bed because it digests very slowly.

1. Add the cottage cheese in a small bowl.

2. Add the blueberries.

3. Add the nutmeg.

4. Drizzle maple syrup over the bowl.

Enjoy!

Snacks	173
Cottage Cheese Daisy, 0.5 cup	110
Organic frozen blueberries Good and gather, 0.5 cup	35
Maple Syrup Bethel, 0.5 Tbsp.	28
Nutmeg Nutmeg, 0.25 tsp	0

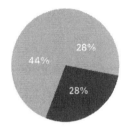

	Total
Carbohydrates (20g)	44%
Fat (5g)	28%
Protein (13g)	28%

Nutrition Facts
Calories 173
Fat 5g
Saturated fat 3g
Carbohydrates 20g
Fiber 2g
Sugar 10g
Protein 13g
Sodium 391mg

Avocado Toast

🍴 SERVES 1

🕐 TOTAL TIME: 5 min

- 1/4 of an avocado
- 1 piece of toast
- Strawberry slices
- Balsamic vinegar– 1/2 teaspoon or 2.5 ml

1. Toast the bread.

2. Mash up the avocado.

Add the avocado to a bowl and mash it with a fork.

3. Spread the avocado on the toast.

4. Add the strawberry slices on the toast.

Now season with salt and pepper.

5. Drizzle balsamic vinegar on toast.

Enjoy!

Snacks		172
Bread Organic Bread, 1 slice		100
Strawberry Banana Slices Kirkland, 3 grams		10
Balsamic, Vinegar Nutritiondata, 0.17 tbsp (16g)		2
Avocado 0.25 medium		60

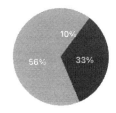

		Total
▨	Carbohydrates (25g)	56%
■	Fat (6g)	33%
▨	Protein (4g)	10%

Nutrition Facts

Calories 172

Fat 6g

Saturated fat 1g

Carbohydrates 25g

Fiber 6g

Sugar 4g

Protein 4g

Sodium 163mg

Homemade Nutella

 SERVES 1

🕐 TOTAL TIME: 5 min

- Unsweetened almond butter- 1 tablespoon or 15g
- Cocoa powder- 1/2 teaspoon or 1g
- Pure maple syrup- 1 teaspoon or 5 ml

Note: You can pair this Nutella with anything. Here are some examples

- Banna
- Almonds
- Crackers
- Strawberries
- Apples
- Grapes
- Toast

1. Add all the ingredients into a small bowl and mix.

Enjoy!

Snacks	110
Unsweetened almond butter Barney Butter, 1 tbsp	90
Cocoa powder 0.5 tsp	2
Maple Syrup Pure, 5 ml	19

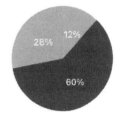

		Total
	Carbohydrates (8g)	28%
	Fat (8g)	60%
	Protein (3g)	12%

Nutrition Facts

Calories 110

Fat 8g

Saturated fat 1g

Carbohydrates 8g

Fiber 0g

Sugar 4g

Protein 3g

Sodium 47mg

Kale Chips

🍴 SERVES 2-3

🕐 TOTAL TIME: 80 min

- Kale- 4oz or 115g
- Olive oil- 1 tablespoon or 15 ml
- Salt to taste

1. Preheat oven to 200°F or 95°C.

2. Remove the kale leaf from the stem.
You can do this with your hands or you can use kitchen shears.

3. Add the kale leaves to a bowl.

4. Drizzle with olive oil and season with salt.
Mix well with your hands.

5. Bake in the oven for 60-75 minutes.
Add the kale to a baking tray and bake until the kale chips are very crisp. Serve and enjoy!

Snacks 159

Kale, raw 40
4 oz

Olive Oil 119
1 tbsp

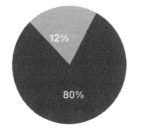

		Total
🟦 Carbohydrates (5g)		12%
🟫 Fat (15g)		80%
🟦 Protein (3g)		8%

Nutrition Facts
Calories 159
Fat 15g
Saturated fat 2g
Carbohydrates 5g
Fiber 5g
Sugar 1g
Protein 3g
Sodium 60mg

Popcorn

🍴 SERVES 3-4

🕐 TOTAL TIME: 15 min

- Popcorn Kernels- 1/4 cup or 32g
- Vegetable oil- 1/2 teaspoon or 2.5 ml
- Salt- 1/4 teaspoon or 1g
- Butter- 1 tablespoon or 15g
- Brown paper lunch bag

Optional- to make this parmesan herb popcorn

- Grated parmesan- 1/4 cup or 25g
- Italian seasoning- 1 teaspoon or .5g

1. Add popcorn to the brown paper bag.

Once the kernels are in the bag, drizzle vegetable oil over them, then fold over the top of the bag 3 times and shake the bag to coat all of the kernels in oil. (do not tape or staple the bag).

2. Add the bag to the microwave.

Microwave for 3-5 minutes, or once the popping slows down to 1-2 pops at a time.

3. Add butter to a microwave-safe bowl.

4. Microwave butter.

Microwave the butter on half power for 30-60 seconds or until the butter is fully melted.

5. Drizzle butter and salt over the popcorn.

Snacks	220
Popcorn Kernels, 0.25 cups	14
Vegetable oil 0.5 tsp	21
Butter, unsalted 1 tbsp	102
Grated Parmesan Grated Parmesan, 4 tbsp	84

		Total
▨ Carbohydrates (3g)		7%
▮ Fat (20g)		82%
▨ Protein (6g)		11%

Nutrition Facts
Calories 220
Fat 20g
Saturated fat 11g
Carbohydrates 3g
Fiber 0g
Sugar 0g
Protein 6g
Sodium 362mg

Homemade Trail Mix

🍴 SERVES 6-8

🕐 TOTAL TIME: 5 min

- Almonds- 1 cup or 96g

- Peanuts- 1 cup or 135g

- Dried cranberries- 1 cup or 120g

- Chocolate chips- 1 cup or 165g

Note: you can switch out any of the nuts for walnuts

or pecans.

1. Mix all the ingredients together and store in a covered container.

Snacks	3,296
Almonds 1 cup, whole	828
Peanuts 1 cup without shells	828
Dried Cranberries Dried cranberries, 1 cup	520
Chocolate Chips Nestlé chocolate chips, 1 cup(s)	1,120

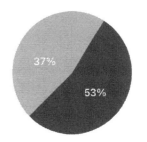

		Total
◼ Carbohydrates (330g)		37%
◼ Fat (207g)		53%
◼ Protein (83g)		9%

Nutrition Facts
Calories 3,296
Fat 207g
Saturated fat 55g
Carbohydrates 330g
Fiber 207g
Sugar 253g
Protein 83g
Sodium 148mg

Rice Cakes

🍴 SERVES 2-3

🕐 TOTAL TIME: 25 min

- White Rice- 1 cup or 230g
- 1 egg
- Parmesan cheese- 1/4 cup or 25g (optional)
- Salt and pepper to taste
- Olive oil- 1 tablespoon or 15 ml

1. Cook rice according to package instructions.

2. Add all of the ingredients (except for the olive oil) to a bowl.

Mix it all together using a fork, spoon, or whatever you have.

3. Form the rice cakes.

Using your hands, form the rice mixture into a circle shape; this mixture should make 2-3 cakes.

4. Add olive oil to a medium preheated pan.

5. Cook the cakes.

Add the rice cakes to the pan and flatten them with a spatula. Cook the first side for 5 minutes or until the bottom turns golden brown. Then flip and cook the second side for 3 minutes or until the bottom turns golden brown. Enjoy!

Snacks	417
White rice, cooked 1 cup	121
Egg 1 large	72
Parmesan cheese 0.25 cup	105
Olive Oil 1 tbsp	119

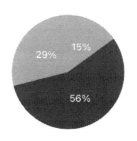

		Total
Carbohydrates (30g)		29%
Fat (25g)		56%
Protein (15g)		15%

Nutrition Facts
Calories 417
Fat 25g
Saturated fat 7g
Carbohydrates 30g
Fiber 0g
Sugar 0g
Protein 15g
Sodium 509mg

Fried Chickpeas

🍴 SERVES 2-3

🕐 TOTAL TIME: 20 min

- Can of chickpeas- 15oz or 425g
- Olive oil- 2 tablespoons or 30 ml
- Pinch of salt and pepper

1. Dry out the chickpeas.

Drain the water from the chickpea can, and then pat the chickpeas dry with a paper towel.

2. Add olive oil to a medium preheated pan.

3. Cook the chickpeas.

Cook on medium heat for about 15 minutes (stirring often) or until the peas turn golden brown.

4. Season with salt and pepper.

Serve and enjoy!

Snacks	736
can of chickpeas Essa, 15 ounce	498
Olive Oil 2 tbsp	239

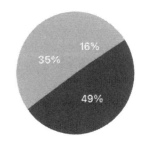

	Total
Carbohydrates (59g)	35%
Fat (36g)	49%
Protein (26g)	16%

Nutrition Facts
Calories 736
Fat 36g
Saturated fat 5g
Carbohydrates 59g
Fiber 0g
Sugar 0g
Protein 26g
Sodium 1mg

Fried Plantains

🍴 SERVES 2

🕐 TOTAL TIME: 10 min

- 2 plantains
- Olive oil- 2 tablespoons or 30 ml
- Salt to taste

1. Prepare the plantains.

Peel the plantains and cut them into 1/4-inch slices.

2. Add olive oil to a medium preheated pan.

3. Fry the plantains.

Cook the plantains for 3-4 minutes or until browned on the first side. Then flip and cook for 1-2 minutes on the second side or until the bottom is golden brown.

4. Season with salt.

Serve and enjoy!

Snacks   669

Plantain Raw Whole
Generic, 2 plantain   430

Olive Oil
2 tbsp   239

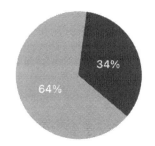

	Total
Carbohydrates (116g)	64%
Fat (27g)	34%
Protein (4g)	2%

Nutrition Facts
Calories 669
Fat 27g
Saturated fat 4g
Carbohydrates 116g
Fiber 6g
Sugar 54g
Protein 4g
Sodium 1mg

Cheese Quesadilla

🍴 SERVES 2-4

🕐 TOTAL TIME: 15 min

- 2 (8-inch) flour tortillas
- Monterey jack cheese- 2/3 cup or 80g
- Olive oil- 4 tablespoons or 60 ml

1. Assemble the Quesadilla.

Add the cheese to one side of each tortilla. Make sure to put everything on one side of the tortilla. After adding everything fold the side with nothing over the side with everything.

2. Brush the outside of each quesadilla with olive oil.

Use a pastry brush to brush about 1 tablespoon of olive oil on each side of the quesadilla.

3. Cook the quesadilla.

In a medium preheated pan, cook the first side of the quesadilla for 2-3 minutes. Then flip the quesadilla and cook the second side for 1 minute. Serve and enjoy!

Snacks	981
8-inch Flour Tortillas, 2 tortilla	240
Monterey Jack Cheese Kroger, 0.66 cup (28g)	264
Olive Oil 4 tbsp	477

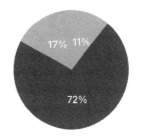

	Total
Carbohydrates (44g)	17%
Fat (80g)	72%
Protein (26g)	11%

Nutrition Facts

Calories 981
Fat 80g
Saturated fat 23g
Carbohydrates 44g
Fiber 4g
Sugar 0g
Protein 26g
Sodium 450mg

Tortilla Chips

🍴 SERVES 2-4

🕐 TOTAL TIME: 20 min

- 4 (8 inch) tortillas
- Vegetable oil spray
- Salt- 1/2 teaspoon or 2g

Optional seasoning

- Italian seasoning- 1 teaspoon or .5g
- Paprika- 1 teaspoon or 4g
- Garlic Powder- 1 teaspoon or 4g

1. Preheat oven to 350°F or 175°C.

Adjust oven racks to the upper and lower middle position (because we will be using two baking trays.

2. Cut the tortillas into 8ths using a pizza cutter or kitchen knife.

3. Spray tortilla wedges generously with vegetable oil.

4. Season with salt and optional seasoning.

Mix the wedges and seasoning together with your hands.

5. Add the wedges to two baking trays.

Do this after lining the trays with baking sheets or tin foil.

6. Bake for 10-15 minutes or until golden brown.

The lower rack may bake slightly faster than the upper rack. Serve and enjoy!

Snacks	728
Tortillas, Flour, 8-Inch Ortega, 4 tortilla	480
Vegetable oil 2 tbsp	248

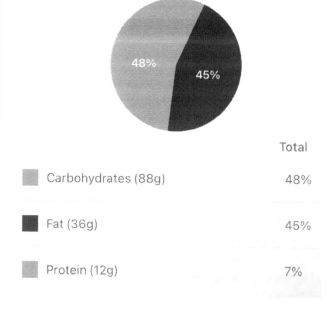

		Total
▢ Carbohydrates (88g)		48%
▢ Fat (36g)		45%
▢ Protein (12g)		7%

Calories 728
Fat 36g
Saturated fat 8g
Carbohydrates 88g
Fiber 4g
Sugar 0g
Protein 12g
Sodium 800mg

Quinoa

SERVES 1

TOTAL TIME: 30 min

- Quinoa- 1/2 cup or 90g
- 6 cherry tomatoes
- Feta cheese- 2 tablespoons or 17g
- Pinch of salt
- Water- 1 cup or 240 ml

Sauce

- Ground turmeric- 1/8 teaspoon or. 25g
- Freshly squeezed lemon juice- 2 tablespoons or 30 ml
- Olive oil- 2 tablespoons or 30 ml
- Pinch of salt and pepper

1. Boil water and add in the quinoa.

In a medium pot, bring 1 cup of water to boil. Now add in the quinoa and a pinch of salt, then reduce the heat to medium-low.

2. Cook the quinoa.

Cook the quinoa for about 15 minutes until the quinoa is tender and the water is absorbed.

3. Transfer the quinoa.

Move the quinoa to a bowl and let it cool.

4. Make the sauce.

Add all of the sauce ingredients to a bowl and mix them together.

5. Cut the cherry tomatoes into halves.

6. Add the tomatoes and sauce to the quinoa bowl.

Sprinkle a little feta cheese over the top and serve.

Quinoa

NUTRITION FACTS

Calories 425

Fat 33g

Saturated fat 6g

Carbohydrates 25g

Fiber 3g

Sugar 5g

Protein 7g

Sodium 227mg

Snacks	425
Quinoa, cooked 0.5 cup	111
Cherry Tomatoes Cherry Tomatoes - 5 Average Size, 6.25 individual	19
Feta cheese 2 tbsp	50
Lemon juice 2 tbsp	7
Olive Oil 2 tbsp	239

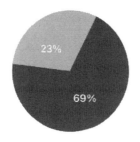

		Total
▉	Carbohydrates (25g)	23%
▉	Fat (33g)	69%
▉	Protein (7g)	7%

Tomato Basil Bites

🍴 SERVES 2-4

🕐 TOTAL TIME: 10 min

- 8 grape or cherry tomatoes
- 8 mozzarella balls
- 8 basil leaves
- Olive oil- 1 tablespoon or 15 ml
- 8 toothpicks- at least 3 inches long

Note: you need 3-inch long toothpicks; regular toothpicks are not long enough. Also, fresh baby mozzarella balls packed in water are the best for this recipe. If you can not find baby mozzarella balls cut the regular mozzarella balls packed in water into 3/4th-inch chunks. Regardless try to get mozzarella balls packed in water.

1. Cut the tomatoes in half.

2. Assemble the bites.

- Slide half of a tomato down a toothpick
- Slide the basil leaf down the toothpick
- Slide the mozzarella ball down the toothpick
- Slide the other half of the tomato down the toothpick

3. Season with salt and pepper.

4. Drizzle olive oil over everything.

Enjoy!

Snacks	**280**
Cherry tomatoes 8 cherry tomato	24
Mozzarella Mini Balls Galbani, 60 g / one ball	136
Olive Oil 1 tbsp	119

	Total
Carbohydrates (5g)	8%
Fat (24g)	75%
Protein (12g)	17%

Nutrition Facts

Calories 280

Fat 24g

Saturated fat 9g

Carbohydrates 5g

Fiber 2g

Sugar 4g

Protein 12g

Sodium 457mg

Candied Pecans

🍴 SERVES 1

🕐 TOTAL TIME: 20 min

- Pecans- 1/2 cup or 65g

Pecan Mixture

- Powdered sugar- 2 tablespoons or 28g
- Ground cinnamon- 1/4 teaspoon or .5g
- Pinch of ground nutmeg
- Pinch of cayenne pepper
- Pinch of salt

1. Preheat oven to 350°F or 175°C.

Line a baking tray with tin foil or parchment paper.

2. Combine the pecan mixture in a bowl.

Mix everything well.

3. Add the pecans to the bowl.

Stir and coat the pecans with the mixture.

4. Add the pecans to a baking tray.

5. Bake the pecans.

Bake for 10 minutes or until the nuts turn dark brown.

Serve and enjoy!

Snacks	528
Pecans Youngs Pecans, 0.5 cup(30g)	420
Sugar Powdered Parkhurst, 2 Tbs	108

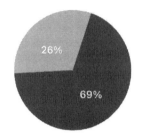

	Total
Carbohydrates (35g)	26%
Fat (42g)	69%
Protein (6g)	5%

Nutrition Facts

Calories 528

Fat 42g

Saturated fat 4g

Carbohydrates 35g

Fiber 4g

Sugar 29g

Protein 6g

Sodium 112mg

Stuffed Jalapeños

🍴 SERVES 2-3

🕐 TOTAL TIME: 25 min

- 6 Jalapeño peppers
- Cooking spray

Filling mixture

- Whipped cream cheese- 1/2 cup or 120 ml
- Cheddar cheese- 2/3 cup or 110g
- 2 scallions (chopped) (see page 19)
- Salt- 1/4 teaspoon or 1g
- Small pinch of pepper

1. Preheat oven to 450°F or 230°C.

2. Cut the jalapeños in half.

Remove the seeds and ribs from the inside. See video below.

Scan Me

3. Finely chop the scallions

See page 19.

4. Make the filling mixture.

Add all of the filling mixture ingredients in a bowl. Then mix everything together. You can use a fork, spoon, whisk, or anything you have lying around the kitchen to mix everything together.

5. Add the filling to the jalapeños.

Add 1 tablespoon of the cream cheese filling into each jalapeño half.

6. Line the baking tray with parchment paper or tin foil.

Then coat the lining with baking spray so the jalapeños do not stick to the baking tray.

7. Add the jalapeños to the baking tray.

8. Bake the jalapeños.

Bake them at 450°F for 10 minutes or until the jalapeños are slightly browned. Serve and enjoy!

Stuffed Jalpeños

NUTRITION FACTS

Calories 367

Fat 40g

Saturated fat 24g

Carbohydrates 18g

Fiber 7g

Sugar 5g

Protein 12g

Sodium 467mg

Snacks	367
Whipped Cream Cheese Giant Whipped Cream Cheese, 0.5 cup(s)	160
Cheddar cheese 0.66 cup(s)	129
Scallions Honeygrow, 1 oz	10
Cooking Spray Crisco, 4 - second spray	20
Jalapeño Pepper Whole, 6 pepper	24

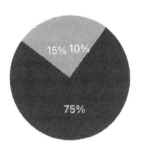

		Total
▢	Carbohydrates (18g)	15%
▨	Fat (40g)	75%
▢	Protein (12g)	10%

Caprese Pizza

 SERVES 1

🕐 TOTAL TIME: 10 min

- 1 slice of pita bread
- Pizza sauce- 1/4 cup or 60 ml
- Mozzarella cheese- 1/2 cup or 40g
- 1/2 a roma tomato sliced (see page 17)
- Chopped basil leaves- 1 tablespoon or 3g
- Balsamic vinegar- 1/2 tablespoon or 8 ml
- Salt and pepper to taste

1. Spread pizza sauce onto pita bread.

2. Sprinkle the cheese onto the sauce.

3. Add the tomato slices.

4. Season with salt and pepper.

5. Microwave for 1 minute.

6. Sprinkle basil and drizzle the balsamic vinegar over the pizza.

Snacks		361
Pita bread		157
1 medium pita		
Sauce		30
Pizza, ¼ th Cup		
Mozzarella Cheese		160
Kraft, 0.5 cup		
Roma tomato		6
0.5 tomato		
Balsamic, Vinegar		7
Nutritiondata, 0.5 tbsp (16g)		
Basil Leaves		1
Fresh Basil, 6.25 leaves, 2.5g		

		Total
Carbohydrates (41g)		45%
Fat (13g)		33%
Protein (20g)		22%

Nutrition Facts

Calories 361

Fat 13g

Saturated fat 7g

Carbohydrates 41g

Fiber 3g

Sugar 6g

Protein 20g

Sodium 899mg

Celery Sticks

 SERVES 1

🕐 TOTAL TIME: 5 min

- Hummus- 1 tablespoon or 15 ml
- 1 celery stick
- 10 Almonds

1. Cut the celery stick into 2-inch increments.

2. Spread hummus in the celery stick.

3. Add in the almonds on top of the hummus.
See the video below to see the full recipe
demonstrated.

Scan Me

Snacks	115
Celery Stick Sainsbury's, 1 Stick	10
Hummus hummus, 1 tbsp	35
Almond - 1 Whole Almond, 10 almond	70

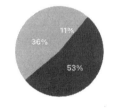

	Total
Carbohydrates (13g)	36%
Fat (8g)	53%
Protein (4g)	11%

Nutrition Facts
Calories 115
Fat 8g
Saturated fat 0g
Carbohydrates 13g
Fiber 13g
Sugar 2g
Protein 4g
Sodium 65mg

Banana Cookies

 SERVES 1

🕐 TOTAL TIME: 25 min

- 2 bananas
- Oats- 1 cup or 90g
- Cinnamon- 1 teaspoon or 2g
- Handful of raisins
- Coconut oil- 2 teaspoons or 9g

1. Preheat oven to 360°F or 180°C.

2. Mash up the bananas.

Add the bananas to a bowl and mash them up.

3. Add the oats, cinnamon, and raisins to the bowl.

Mix everything in the bowl.

4. Form the mix into small circles.

5. Add parchment paper or tin foil to a baking tray.

6. Add the coconut oil to the parchment paper or tin foil and spread it around.

This is so the cookies don't stick to the paper.

7. Bake at 360°F or 180°C for 15-20 minutes.

Snacks	622
Banana 2 medium	210
Oatmeal, dry 1 cup	307
Raisins Sunmade Raisins, 0.33 oz	30
Coconut oil 2 tsp	75

	Total
Carbohydrates (116g)	71%
Fat (15g)	21%
Protein (13g)	8%

Nutrition Facts
Calories 622
Fat 15g
Saturated fat 9g
Carbohydrates 116g
Fiber 15g
Sugar 36g
Protein 13g
Sodium 9mg

Sides

Green Beans

🍴 SERVES 4-5

🕐 TOTAL TIME: 25 min

- Green Beans- 1 lb or 455g
- 3 garlic cloves (minced) (see page 16)
- Olive oil- 1 tablespoon or 15 ml
- Salt- 1/4 teaspoon or 1g
- Pepper- 1/4 teaspoon or .5g
- Water- 1/4 cup or 60 ml
- Butter- 1 tablespoon or 15g

1. (Optional) Trim the ends off the green beans.
I use a chef's knife.

2. Add the olive oil to a large medium preheated pan.

3. Cook the green beans.
Add the green beans, and season with salt and pepper. Then cook for 4-6 minutes (stirring occasionally).

4. Add water and cover the skillet.
Leave the skillet covered for about 2 minutes or until the green beans turn light green.

5. Remove the lid and turn the heat up to medium-high.
Cook the green beans (stirring occasionally) until the water evaporates, which should be about 1 minute.

6. Add the butter and minced garlic.

After adding everything in, stir often for about 2-4 minutes or until the green beans are lightly browned. Serve and enjoy!

Snacks	372
Green bean 1 lb	141
Garlic Clove ~ 4g per average clove Fresh, 3 clove	12
Olive Oil 1 tbsp	119
Butter Unsalted Butter, 1 tbsp	100

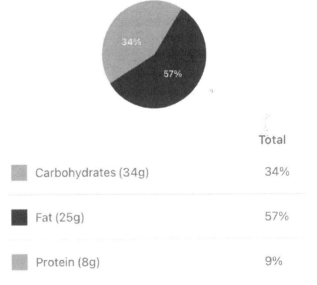

	Total
Carbohydrates (34g)	34%
Fat (25g)	57%
Protein (8g)	9%

Nutrition Facts
Calories 372
Fat 25g
Saturated fat 8g
Carbohydrates 34g
Fiber 14g
Sugar 9g
Protein 8g
Sodium 175mg

Roasted Broccoli

🍴 SERVES 3-4

🕐 TOTAL TIME: 20 min

- Broccoli- 6 cups or 450g
- Olive oil- 1/4 cup or 60 ml
- Salt- 1/4 teaspoon or 1g
- Pinch of pepper
- Juice from 1 lemon (optional)

1. Preheat oven to 450°F or 230°C.

2. Whisk together the olive oil, salt, and pepper in a large bowl.

3. Add the broccoli to the bowl.

Toss the broccoli with your hands until the broccoli is evenly coated with the oil.

4. Add the broccoli to a baking tray.

Line the tray with parchment paper or tin foil.

5. Bake the broccoli.

Bake for 10 minutes or until lightly browned.

6. Optional

Squeeze the juice from one lemon over the broccoli. Enjoy!

Snacks	657
Olive oil 4 tbsp	477
Broccoli 6 cup, chopped or diced	180

	Total
Carbohydrates (35g)	20%
Fat (56g)	72%
Protein (14g)	8%

Nutrition Facts

Calories 657
Fat 56g
Saturated fat 8g
Carbohydrates 35g
Fiber 14g
Sugar 9g
Protein 14g
Sodium 175mg

Microwaved Sweet Potato

🍴 SERVES 2

🕐 TOTAL TIME: 15 min

- 1 sweet potato
- Butter- 1 teaspoon or 5g
- Salt and pepper to taste

Optional

- Brown sugar- 1 tablespoon or 11g

1. Rinse off your potato.

2. Poke 8-10 holes in your potato with a fork.

Do this so the potato does not explode in the microwave. See video below.

Scan Me

3. Microwave potato for 10 minutes.

At the halfway point, flip the sweet potato over. Microwave time will depend on the thickness of your potato. The potato is done once you can easily stick a fork into the center of the potato with no resistance.

4. Open up the potato

Split open the potato lengthwise. Then, pop the potato open by pressing the two sides of the potato in lightly. See the video below to see step 4 demonstrated.

Scan Me

5. Add in the butter

Mix it all up with the inside of the potato. Then season with salt and pepper. Add in the optional brown sugar if you want a sweeter potato. Enjoy!

Microwaved Sweet Potato

NUTRITION FACTS

Calories 231

Fat 10g

Saturated fat 4g

Carbohydrates 34g

Fiber 4g

Sugar 17g

Protein 2g

Sodium 310mg

Snacks	231
Sweet potato 1 medium, 5 inch long	164
Butter Organic Butter, 1 tsp(s)	33
Brown sugar 3 tsp, unpacked	34

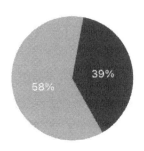

	Total
Carbohydrates (34g)	58%
Fat (10g)	39%
Protein (2g)	3%

Roasted Potatoes

🍴 SERVES 4-6

🕐 TOTAL TIME: 45 min

- Red potatoes- 1 lb or 455g
- Olive oil- 1 tablespoon or 15 ml
- Salt- 1/4 teaspoon or 1g
- Pinch of pepper

1. Preheat oven to 450°F or 230°C.

2. Slice the red potatoes in half.

3. Mix the olive oil, salt, and pepper together in a large bowl.

4. Add the potatoes to the bowl.

Mix with your hands until the potatoes are coated evenly with the olive oil.

5. Add the potatoes to a baking tray.

Line the baking tray with parchment paper or tin foil before adding the potatoes.

6. Bake the potatoes.

Bake them for 30-35 minutes or until the skin is spotted brown. Serve and enjoy!

Snacks	523
Red Potatoes Potatoes, 1 lb(s)	404
Olive oil 1 tbsp	119

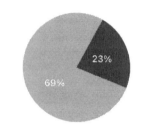

		Total
Carbohydrates (88g)		69%
Fat (13g)		23%
Protein (10g)		8%

Nutrition Facts
Calories 523
Fat 13g
Saturated fat 2g
Carbohydrates 88g
Fiber 8g
Sugar 6g
Protein 10g
Sodium 524mg

Garlic Bread

🍴 SERVES 5-7

🕐 TOTAL TIME: 25 min

- 1 loaf of French bread

Spread

- Garlic butter- 8 tablespoons or 120g
- Parmesan cheese- 1/4 cup or 25g
- Chopped Parsley- 1 tablespoon or 1g

1. Preheat oven to 350°F or 175°C.

2. Cut the french bread in half vertically.

3. Make the garlic butter spread.

Add the spread ingredients into a bowl and mix together well. I recommend using a fork to mix.

4. Spread the mixture to both cut sides of the bread.

5. Wrap each half of the bread in tin foil.

6. Bake for 15-20 minutes.

Serve and enjoy!

Snacks	865
Garlic Butter Chef Shamy Garlic Butter, 8 tablespoon	480
Italian Parsley (Raw) Parsley, 1 Tbs	1
Parmesan cheese 0.25 cup	105
French Bread French Bread (Publix), 3.2 Oz	278

	Total
▨ Carbohydrates (57g)	28%
■ Fat (59g)	65%
▨ Protein (15g)	7%

Nutrition Facts
Calories 865
Fat 59g
Saturated fat 37g
Carbohydrates 57g
Fiber 2g
Sugar 0g
Protein 15g
Sodium 2,300mg

Garlic Mushrooms

🍴 SERVES 2

🕐 TOTAL TIME: 20 min

- Baby Bella mushrooms- 1 lb or 455g
- Salt and pepper to taste
- Butter- 1 tablespoon or 15g
- Olive oil- 1 tablespoon or 15 ml
- 1 medium onion, diced (see page 16)
- Apple Juice- 2 tablespoons or 30 ml
- 4 cloves of garlic, minced (see page 16)
- Fresh parsley chopped- 2 tablespoons or 2g
- Thyme- 1 tablespoon or 4g

1. Cut the bigger mushrooms in half.

You can leave the small ones as they are
See the video below.

Scan Me

2. Add the butter and olive oil to a preheated medium pan.

Add in the olive oil first then throw in the butter and let it fully melt.

3. Cook the onion for 1-2 minutes.

Or until they turn slightly brown.

4. Add in the mushrooms.

Add the mushrooms in with the onions and cook for about 4 minutes. Stir occasionally, but not too much; you want to let the mushrooms sit untouched for 1-minute increments.

5. Add the apple juice and season with salt and pepper to taste.

Stir everything together and cook for about 2 minutes.

6. Add in the garlic thyme and parsley.

After adding them all in, stir and cook for about 30 seconds. Your mushrooms are done; enjoy!

If you are enjoying the book, an honest review would be greatly appreciated!

Scan Me

Garlic Mushrooms

NUTRITION FACTS

Calories 429

Fat 24g

Saturated fat 9g

Carbohydrates 37g

Fiber 9g

Sugar 16g

Protein 19g

Sodium 107mg

Snacks	429
Baby Bella Mushrooms Monterey, 1 lb(s)	107
Organic Butter Horizon, 1 tbs	100
Olive Oil 1 tbsp	119
White onion 1 large	60
Apple Juice Juice, 1 oz	14
Garlic 4 clove	18
Parsley, dried 2 tbsp	9
Thyme, fresh 3 tsp	2

		Total
▇	Carbohydrates (37g)	33%
▇	Fat (24g)	50%
▇	Protein (19g)	17%

Avocado Salad

 SERVES 1

🕐 TOTAL TIME: 10 min

- 1 avocado, diced (see page 19)
- 1 Roma tomato, diced (see page 17)
- 1/4 a red onion, diced (see page 16)
- Juice from 1 lime
- Chopped cilantro- 2 tablespoons or 1g

1. Mix the avocado, Roma tomato, red onion, and cilantro in a small mixing bowl, then add in lime juice.

Go to the following pages if you do not know how to dice the following ingredients:

Avocado- 19

Tomato- 17

Red Onion- 16

Snacks	272
Avocado 1 medium	240
Roma tomato 1 tomato	11
Red onion 0.25 medium	11
Lime juice - Raw 1 lime yields	10

	Total
Carbohydrates (21g)	28%
Fat (22g)	67%
Protein (4g)	5%

Nutrition Facts
Calories 272
Fat 22g
Saturated fat 3g
Carbohydrates 21g
Fiber 11g
Sugar 4g
Protein 4g
Sodium 15mg

Coleslaw

🍴 SERVES 2

🕐 TOTAL TIME: 10 min

- 1 bag of coleslaw mix- about 14 oz or 395g

Coleslaw sauce

- Mayonnaise- 1/2 cup or 120 ml

- Sugar- 2 tablespoons or 28g

- Freshly squeezed lemon juice- 2 tablespoons or 30 ml

- Distilled vinegar- 1 tablespoon or 15 ml

- Salt- 1/4 teaspoon or 1g

- Black pepper- 1/2 teaspoon or 1g

1. Make the sauce.

Add the coleslaw sauce ingredients into a bowl and mix everything well.

2. Add the coleslaw mix into the bowl.

Mix everything well.

3. Refrigerate overnight.

Chill in an airtight container.

Snacks	968
Coleslaw mix - bag Kroger, 14 ounce	117
Mayonnaise 0.5 cup	748
Lemon juice, raw 2 tbsp(s)	7
Sugar 2 tbsp	97

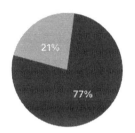

		Total
Carbohydrates (51g)		21%
Fat (82g)		77%
Protein (5g)		2%

Nutrition Facts

Calories 968

Fat 82g

Saturated fat 13g

Carbohydrates 51g

Fiber 9g

Sugar 41g

Protein 5g

Sodium 816mg

Moroccan Couscous

🍴 SERVES 2

🕐 TOTAL TIME: 15 min

- Water - 2 1/2 cups or 600 ml
- Olive oil- 2 tablespoons or 30 ml
- Salt- 1/2 teaspoon or 2g
- Pepper to taste
- Morrocan couscous- 2 cups or 340g
- 2 minced garlic cloves (see page 16)

Note: There are 2 types of couscous-

Morrocan couscous- which is the smaller and more common form of couscous.

Israeli or Pearl couscous- this is the larger type and takes slightly longer to cook.

The first recipe will use Moroccan couscous; the second will use Israeli couscous.

1. Cook the garlic.

Add the olive oil to a medium preheated **pot** and saute the garlic for 60-90 seconds.

2. Add the water with the garlic and bring it to a boil.

Season with salt before the water gets to a boil.

3. Turn off the heat once the water comes to a boil, then add in couscous.

After turning off the heat, immediately add in the couscous.

4. Cover the pan with a lid.

Let the pan sit untouched for 5 minutes.

5. Fluff couscous with a fork and serve!

Remove the lid, fluff the couscous, and season with salt and pepper. Enjoy!

Morocan Couscous

NUTRITION FACTS

Calories 600

Fat 27g

Saturated fat 4g

Carbohydrates 74g

Fiber 5g

Sugar 0g

Protein 12g

Sodium 18mg

Snacks	600
Olive Oil 2 tbsp	239
Couscous couscous, 2 cup	352
Garlic 2 clove	9

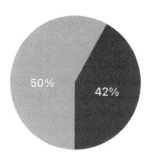

		Total
	Carbohydrates (74g)	50%
	Fat (27g)	42%
	Protein (12g)	8%

Pearl Couscous

🍴 SERVES 2

🕐 TOTAL TIME: 20 min

- Water- 3 cups or 720 ml
- Olive oil- 2 tablespoons or 30 ml
- Salt- 1/2 teaspoon or 2g
- Pepper to taste
- Pearl couscous- 2 cups or 290g
- 2 minced garlic cloves (see page 16)

1. Cook the garlic.

Add the olive oil to a medium preheated **pot** and saute the garlic for 60-90 seconds.

2. Add the water with the garlic and bring it to a boil.

Season with salt before the water gets to a boil.

3. Turn the pan's heat down to medium.

Do this right after the water comes to a boil.

4. Add in the couscous and let it simmer for 10 minutes, uncovered.

5. Turn off the heat

6. Cover the pan with a lid

Let the pan sit untouched for 5 minutes.

7. Fluff couscous with a fork and serve!

Snacks	600
Olive Oil 2 tbsp	239
Couscous couscous, 2 cup	352
Garlic 2 clove	9

		Total
🟦 Carbohydrates (74g)		50%
⬛ Fat (27g)		42%
🟦 Protein (12g)		8%

Nutrition Facts

Calories 600

Fat 27g

Saturated fat 4g

Carbohydrates 74g

Fiber 5g

Sugar 0g

Protein 12g

Sodium 18mg

Desserts

Baked Pineapple

🍴 SERVES 2-3

🕐 TOTAL TIME: 30 min

- As many store-bought pineapple slices as you want - 1/2 inch thick or 13 mm thick

Seasoning
- Brown sugar- 2 tablespoons or 22g
- Cinnamon- 1/4 teaspoon or .5g

Note: Slice the thicker store-bought pineapple slices in half. Each pineapple slice should be around 1/2 inch thick.

1. Preheat oven to 400°F or 205°C.

2. Add the seasoning to a bowl and mix together.

3. Coat pineapple slices in the seasoning.
Drop each pineapple slice into the seasoning and fully coat both sides.

4. Line a baking tray with tin foil and add the pineapple slices.

5. Bake for 20-25 minutes. Flip at the halfway point. See the video to see how the pineapple should look before flipping.

Scan Me

6. Enjoy!
If your pineapple is still tart, put it back in the oven for a few minutes. The cooking time will vary depending on the ripeness of the pineapple.

Snacks	248
Brown sugar 6 tsp, unpacked	68
Slices Pineapple slices, 6 slices	180

100%

	Total
Carbohydrates (62g)	100%
Fat (0g)	0%
Protein (0g)	0%

Nutrition Facts
Calories 248
Fat 0g
Saturated fat 0g
Carbohydrates 62g
Fiber 3g
Sugar 59g
Protein 0g
Sodium 35mg

Hot Chocolate

 SERVES 1

🕐 TOTAL TIME: 10 min

- Whole milk- 1.5 cups or 360 ml
- Dark chocolate chips- 1/3 cup or 50g
- Sugar- 1 tablespoon or 14g
- Pinch of salt
- As many marshmallows as you want

1. Add the whole milk and chocolate to a cold pot.

2. Turn the heat up to medium.

3. Stir everything continuously until the chocolate melts.

4. Add in the sugar.

Add in the sugar once the chocolate has fully melted. Stir for 1- 2 minutes.

5. Add a pinch of salt.

Give the pot a few more stirs, then take the pot off the heat.

6. Serve in a cup with small marshmallows. Enjoy!

Snacks	384
Milk, whole 1.5 cup	223
Dark Chocolate Chocolate Chip Gifford's, 0.33 cup	112
Sugar 1 tbsp	49

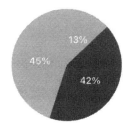

	Total
Carbohydrates (44g)	45%
Fat (18g)	42%
Protein (12g)	13%

Nutrition Facts
Calories 384
Fat 18g
Saturated fat 11g
Carbohydrates 44g
Fiber 1g
Sugar 44g
Protein 12g
Sodium 214mg

Peach Sorbet

🍴 SERVES 1

🕐 TOTAL TIME: 5 min

- Frozen peaches- 3.5 cups or 455g
- Honey- 1/4 cup or 60 ml

1. Add the peaches and honey to a high powered blender or food processor and blend for 1-2 minutes on high.

2. Add the sorbet to a loaf pan.

3. Freeze overnight.

Snacks   452

Frozen Peaches   194
Wegmans, 1 lb(s)

Honey   258
0.25 cup

97%

	Total
Carbohydrates (112g)	97%
Fat (0g)	0%
Protein (3g)	3%

Nutrition Facts
Calories 452
Fat 0g
Saturated fat 0g
Carbohydrates 112g
Fiber 7g
Sugar 99g
Protein 3g
Sodium 3mg

Protein Lava Cake

🍴 SERVES 1

🕐 TOTAL TIME: 20 min

- Oat flour- 2 tablespoons or 10g
- Cocoa powder-1 teaspoon or 1g
- 1 scoop or about 25g of protein powder (preferably chocolate)
- Baking powder- 1/4 teaspoon or .5g
- Apple Sauce- 2 tablespoons or 30 ml
- Almond milk- 2 tablespoons or 30 ml
- 2 bits of dark chocolate (I use Hershey)
- Pinch of salt

If you have a blender, I highly recommend making homemade oat flour; it is really easy. All you have to do is blend up the oats on high power for 30 seconds - 1 minute. Watch the video below to see how I make it.

Scan Me

1. Preheat your oven to 400°F or 205°C.

2. Add all the following ingredients in a ramekin or small bowl. In this order.

1. Oat flour
2. Cocoa powder
3. Protein powder
4. Salt
5. Baking powder
6. Apple Sauce
7. Almond milk

Then mix.

If you do not have a ramekin, make sure your bowl is oven safe. Look for the oven-safe symbol on the bottom of the bowl before tossing it in the oven. The symbol should look something like this.

3. Stir everything together, then add the chocolate bits and a pinch of salt.

4. Bake at 400°F or 205°C for 15 minutes. Enjoy!

Protein Chocolate Lava Cake

NUTRITION FACTS

Calories 213

Fat 3g

Saturated fat 1g

Carbohydrates 19g

Fiber 2g

Sugar 4g

Protein 26g

Sodium 145mg

Snacks	213
Whey Protein Isolate Golden Standard 100%WHEY, 31 g	120
Oat Flour 2 tbsp	53
Cocoa powder 1 tsp	4
Almond Milk Great Value Almond Milk, 0.12 cup	4
Hershey chocolate Hershey mini bar, 0.33 pieces	21
Baking powder 0.25 tsp	1
Apple Sauce Mott's Original Apple Sauce, 0.12 cup (113g)	11

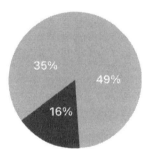

		Total
▨	Carbohydrates (19g)	35%
▨	Fat (3g)	16%
▨	Protein (26g)	49%

Chocolate Mousse

🍴 SERVES 5-10

🕐 TOTAL TIME: 20 min

- Semisweet chocolate chips- 1 cup or 165g
- Water- 1/3 cup or 80 ml
- Heavy cream 1 cup or 240 ml
- 2 Eggs
- Sugar- 2 tablespoons or 28g

1. Melt the Chocolate.

First, add 1 cup of chocolate chips and 1/3 cup of water into a bowl. Then add the bowl on top of a medium-high preheated pot. Make sure to use a glass bowl and not a plastic bowl (so it doesn't melt). See the video below if you are confused.

Scan Me

2. Whisk the heavy cream.

When whisking, do not whisk it too much; only whisk for about 30-60 seconds; we are going for a light and soft cream. See the video below.

Scan Me

3. Crack the eggs and separate the yolk from the egg whites.

Have 2 separate bowls, one for the egg whites and one for the egg yolks.
Only save 1 of the egg yolks.

4. Whisk the egg whites with the sugar.

Whisk together two egg whites. As you whisk the egg whites, slowly add sugar in (I do 1/2 a tablespoon at a time). Whisk them really well till you get a fluffy meringue. See the video if you are confused at all.

Scan Me

5. **Add 1 egg yolk to the melted chocolate and mix together.**

6. **Add the chocolate with the heavy cream.**

Mix it together.

7. **Add the Meringue to the chocolate and cream.**

Add in half the meringue and mix it together with everything. Then after mixing the first half, add in the rest of the meringue and mix together.

8. **Cool in the fridge for at least 4 hours.**

Enjoy!

Nutrition Facts
Calories 1,553
Fat 103g
Saturated fat 61g
Carbohydrates 173g
Fiber 16g
Sugar 157g
Protein 29g
Sodium 153mg

Snacks	1,553
Chocolate Chips, Semi-Sweet Kirkland Signature, 1 cup(s)	960
Heavy Cream 1 cup, whipped	408
Brown Eggs Cage Free Eggs, 1 each	70
Egg White White Egg - Egg White Only, 1 lg	18
Sugar 2 tbsp	97

	Total
Carbohydrates (173g)	39%
Fat (103g)	54%
Protein (29g)	6%

Kitchen Staples

Salsa

🍴 SERVES 2-3

🕐 TOTAL TIME: 10 min

- Roma tomato- 1 lb or 455g
- 1/2 of a small red onion diced (see page 17)
- 1 jalapeño pepper
- Cilantro (chopped)- 1/4 cup or 2g
- Lime juice- 1 tablespoon or 15 ml
- Pinch of salt

1. Dice the tomatoes (see page 17).

2. Dice the onion (see page 16).

3. Dice the Jalapeño.

Scan Me

4. Mix all of the ingredients in a bowl.
Add in the cilantro and lime juice as well.

5. Season everything with salt.

Snacks	103
roma tomatoes fresh tomatoes, 1 lb(s)	68
Pepper Jalapeño, 1 jalapeño	5
Red onion 0.5 medium	22
Lime juice, raw (SS USDA) Generic, 1 fl oz (30.8g)	8

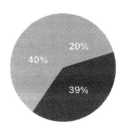

▪ Carbohydrates (18g)		40%
▪ Fat (7g)		39%
▪ Protein (9g)		20%

Nutrition Facts
Calories 103
Fat 7g
Saturated fat 0g
Carbohydrates 18g
Fiber 7g
Sugar 5g
Protein 9g
Sodium 30mg

Guacamole

SERVES 4

🕐 TOTAL TIME: 10 min

- 3 avocados
- 1 lime
- 2 diced Roma tomatoes (see page 17)
- Chopped cilantro- 2 tablespoons or 1g

1. Scoop out the avocado and put it into a bowl.

Discard the pit and skins.

2. Add lime juice to the bowl.

Cut the lime in half and squeeze out all the juice. Optional you can add 1/4 teaspoon of lime zest into the bowl if you have a grater.

3. Whisk the bowl.

Whisk the bowl until the mixture is relatively smooth (leaving some large-sized avocado chunks to stay).

4. Add the tomato and cilantro to the bowl.

Mix everything up and serve!

Snacks	750
Avocado 3 medium	720
Chopped Tomato - Roma Tomato Roma Tomato, 2 whole (62g)	22
Lime juice, raw (SS USDA) Generic, 1 fl oz (30.8g)	8

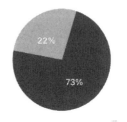

▨ Carbohydrates (45g)	22%
■ Fat (66g)	73%
▨ Protein (10g)	5%

Nutrition Facts

Calories 750

Fat 66g

Saturated fat 10g

Carbohydrates 45g

Fiber 32g

Sugar 7g

Protein 10g

Sodium 38mg

Hummus

🍴 SERVES 4

🕐 TOTAL TIME: 10 min

- 1 can of chickpeas- 15 oz or 425g
- Tahini- 1/4 cup or 60 ml
- 1 garlic clove minced (see page 16)
- Lemon juice- 2 tablespoons or 30 ml
- Salt- 1/4 teaspoon or 1g
- Olive oil- 2 tablespoons or 30 ml

Seasoning

- Paprika- 1/2 teaspoon or 2g

1. Drain the liquid from the chickpea can.

Reserve 1/4 cup or 60 ml of the liquid.

2. Blend the tahini and olive oil.

Add the tahini and olive oil to a blender or food processor and blend on high for 1 minute or until smooth.

3. Add the chickpeas, chickpea liquid, lemon juice, garlic, and salt to the blender.

Blend on high for 30 seconds or until desired texture.

4. Garnish with paprika and serve.

Snacks	812
Chick Peas Can Delmaine, 1 can	205
Tahini 0.25 cup	357
Garlic 1 clove	4
Olive Oil 2 tbsp	239
Lemon juice 2 tbsp	7

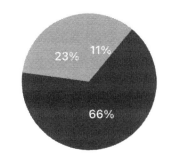

		Total
Carbohydrates (48g)		23%
Fat (61g)		66%
Protein (23g)		11%

Nutrition Facts
Calories 812
Fat 61g
Saturated fat 9g
Carbohydrates 48g
Fiber 8g
Sugar 0g
Protein 23g
Sodium 903mg

Queso

🍴 SERVES 5-7

🕐 TOTAL TIME: 20 min

- Vegetable oil- 1 tablespoon or 15 ml
- 1/2 medium onion, diced (see page 16)
- 1 Jalapeño, diced
- Salt to taste
- 2 cloves of minced garlic (see page 16)
- 1 Roma tomato (diced) See page (17)
- Grated American cheese- .35 lb or 170g
- Grated pepper jack cheese- .125 lb or 58g
- Whole milk- 1/2 cup or 120 ml
- Chopped cilantro- 2 tablespoons or 1g

1. Saute the onions and jalapeño.

Add 1 tablespoon of vegetable oil to a preheated medium-heat **pot**. Then add in the diced onion and jalapeños. Saute (occasionally mixing everything up) for 5-6 minutes or until the veggies become soft. Scan the QR code if you do not know how to dice a jalapeño.

Scan Me

2. Add in the garlic.

Once the onion and jalapeños are softened, add in the garlic. Mix everything together and saute for another 1-2 minutes.

3. Add in the tomato.

Once the garlic starts to get a little color to it, add in the diced tomato. Mix everything together and saute for 45-60 seconds.

4. Add in the cheese and milk.

Once everything is done sauteing, add in both kinds of cheese. Then add in the milk. Stir everything constantly until the cheese is fully melted and the queso has a smooth consistency.

5. Add in the cilantro.

Once the queso has a smooth consistency, add in the cilantro and season to taste with salt. Enjoy!

Queso

NUTRITION FACTS

Calories 917

Fat 74g

Saturated fat 33g

Carbohydrates 27g

Fiber 2g

Sugar 13g

Protein 39g

Sodium 2,719mg

Snacks	917
Vegetable oil 1 tbsp	124
Onion 0.5 medium	22
Jalapeño 1 whole	5
Garlic 2 clove	9
Roma tomato 1 tomato	11
American cheese 0.35 lb	581
pepper jack cheese pepper jack cheesr, 0.12 lb(s)	90
Milk, whole 0.5 cup	74
Cilantro 2 tbsp	0

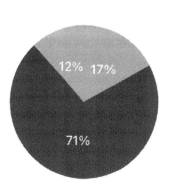

▨	Carbohydrates (27g)	12%
◼	Fat (74g)	71%
▨	Protein (39g)	17%

Made in the USA
Middletown, DE
07 September 2024

60574089R00113